Missions as the Theology of the Church

Copyright 2015 Klaus Fiedler

All rights reserved. No part of this publication may be reproduced, stored in a retrieval system, or transmitted in any from or by any means, electronic, mechanical, photocopying, recording or otherwise without prior permission from the publishers.

Published by

Mzuni Press

P/Bag 201 Luwinga

Mzuzu 2

www.mzunipress.luviri.com

www.mzunipress.blogspot.com

www.africanbookscollective.com

ISBN 978-99960-27-03-1

Mzuni Texts no. 2

Mzuni Press is represented outside Africa by:
African Books Collective Oxford (orders@africanbookscollective.com)

Cover picture: "The Painting of the First Fruits" by Johann Valentin Haidt (1748) shows those who had been baptized during the first 15 years of Moravian missionary work and who had been called to glory by then and are seen to surround Christ with their palm branches as a sign of victory. A copy of the picture is in Herrnhut and still invites to prayer. For details on its history see: "Bruder Chingachgook. Die Herrnhuter Indinanermission and Coopers Lederstrumpf-Romane," *Sächsische Heimatblätter* 4/2006:

Missions as the Theology of the Church

An Argument from Malawi

Klaus Fiedler

Mzuni Press

Mzuni Texts no. 2

Mzuni Press
Mzuzu
2015

To Louise Pirouet, who taught me Church History

A Pamphlet

This book, small as it is, is important for me as it reflects some of my thinking and of my work in missiology. It is now over 25 years that I have been teaching missiological subjects in one form or another, and in those years two themes came up again and again: The relationship between "church" and "mission" and the relationship between the Evangelical missions and those of the other branches of the Christian missionary enterprise, especially the missions of the Great Awakening which I call the "Classical Missions."

This book is neither a monograph nor an extended essay. For a monograph, the depth is insufficient, for an essay too much work has gone into it. So I wrote it as a pamphlet. In a pamphlet one presents ideas for public discussion and reaction. A pamphlet is heartfelt, but far from final. A pamphlet takes the liberty of expressing ideas sometimes a little forcefully, and sometimes it speaks "shorthand." A pamphlet has the freedom to occasionally provoke a smile (a little sarcasm may help in that sometimes) and or more serious reactions.

My pamphlet, covering 2000 years in a sweep, can not be based all on primary sources, but it is in no way devoid of them. Uneven as it is, I present this pamphlet as a first step for what, hopefully, may become a longer book one day. So I welcome the reactions of my students, my colleagues and anyone interested in missiology.

Klaus Fiedler
25.1.2015

For your reactions:
    fiedler42@gmail.com or klaus.fiedler@etf.edu
    P/Bag 201, Luwinga, Mzuzu 2, Malawi

Contents

1 The Centre of all Theology — 7
2 My Background — 7
3 My Presuppositions — 8
    3.1 I Write as an Evangelical — 8
    3.2 Personal Faith is the Centre — 8
    3.3 The Church Came (and still Comes) after the Mission — 8
    3.4 Missions are the Children of Revivals — 9
    3.5 Kenneth Scott Latourette — 9
    3.6 Missiology and other Fields of Theology — 10
    3.7 Modalities – Sodalities — 11
    3.8 The Characteristics of Revivals — 12
4 The First 1600 Years — 15
    4.1 The Sodalities — 16
    4.2 The Missions — 17
5. The Reformations — 18
6 Pietists, Puritans and Orthodox Theologians — 19
7 The Enlightenment — 22
8 The Great Awakening — 23
    8.1 The Awakening — 23
    8.2 The Missions — 27
9 The Restorationist Interlude — 30
10 The Holiness Revival (Second Evangelical Awakening) and the Faith Missions — 33
11 And then Came the Pentecostals — 37
12 A New Evangelical Beginning — 38
13 And then the Charismatics — 38
14 Edinburgh 1910/2010 — 42
    14.1 Evangelicals and the Ecumenical Missions — 44
15 Missions as the Theology of the Church and Predestination — 46
17 The Position of Women in the Kingdom of God — 48
18 Missions as Theology of the Church and Christian Unity — 51
19 What about "Wholistic Mission?" — 54
20 Migration and the Unity of the Church — 54
21 Keep the Revival — 55
Bibliography — 56
    Unpublished — 56
    Published — 56
Louise Pirouet — 61
    Celebrating the Life of Louise Pirouet — 61

1 The Centre of all Theology

Theology is a comprehensive and quite diverse science, and all its departments must be taken seriously. Therefore it may be useful to ask where the centre of theology is, a centre to which all else relates. A typical Lutheran theologian may well answer: The centre, of course, is the doctrine of justification. I can imagine that an Orthodox theologian might say, equally convinced, that the centre is the incarnation, God becoming man. And Robert Moffat, a Congregationalist with a Presbyterian theology, may well have answered: The centre is God's glory.[1] I think that all three answers are correct,[2] but I still prefer to give a different one.[3] While the three answers define the centre of theology in dogmatic terms, I would like to give a more functional definition of that same centre. I do not want to replace those definitions by a better one, but I want to present another perspective, and I will do it by going through the whole course of church history. Before I do that, I want to indicate who I am and clarify the assumptions on which I base my argument.[4]

2 My Background

I write as a missiologist. I received my theological training at the Baptist Seminary in Hamburg, though I learnt no missiology there. It was in Kampala at Makerere University that I discovered that I could be a scholar. Originally I wanted to concentrate on general missiology, maybe on how the Christian faith finds a home in matrilineal societies, but the teaching of Louise Pirouet at Makerere converted

---

[1] Robert and Mary Moffat were pioneer missionaries among the Tswana, in Kuruman, in what is today South Africa. For Robert Moffat's theology see: Bruce Ritchie, The Theology of Robert Moffat of Kuruman, PhD, University of Malawi, 2006.

[2] I do not like the (recently) frequently given answer, that liberation is the centre of the Gospel, as too many liberations are given a home under the same roof. An extreme—but still fascinating—variant was the conviction that God (at least for a time) had set aside the churches in China in order to work with the Cultural Revolution of Chairman Mao Dse Dong (at that time still Mao Tse Tung in the West) more effectively for the Liberation of the Chinese. The problem only was that the Chinese were not aware of that blessing.

[3] After writing the book I found out that Alexander Duff shared my opinion: Andrew F. Walls, "Three Hundred Years of Scottish Missions," in Kenneth R. Ross (ed), *Roots and Fruits. Retrieving Scotland's Missionary Story*, Oxford: Regnum, 2014, p. 35f.

[4] I consolidated my thinking on this topic first in a presentation to the 25th anniversary of the Association of German Speaking Evangelical Missiologists (AfeM) in St Chrischona, published as Klaus Fiedler, "Mission als Theologie der Kirche und Missionen als Kinder der Erweckung," *Evangelikale Missiologie* (27), 2/2011, pp. 61-78.

me to become a [missionary] historian. That was almost 50 years ago, and I have remained a (mission/church) historian ever since.

I am getting older now, but since I expect to still have some years to work and write, it may be too early to write my final will. Still, I want to write, in all humility, a personal book, giving my personal interpretation of church history, pointing out my observation and including, where appropriate, the results of the research of my students. I do not want to present a new missiology, improving on and superseding all those that came before me, but I want to make my own contribution.

3 My Presuppositions

3.1 I Write as an Evangelical

All my theological work I have done as an Evangelical. I never defined my theology in contrast to any other theology, but quite positively: For me Evangelical theology is defined by five emphases: (1) The love of the Bible (and the habit to take it seriously), (2) Emphasis on the personal confession of faith (conversion) (3) Emphasis on mission(s) (or evangelism), (4) the "translation" of personal faith into action and (5) the fellowship of all who believe in Jesus Christ as their Saviour and Lord.

3.2 Personal Faith is the Centre

I see the message of salvation as the centre of the Bible, with conversion and discipleship being the required response. John 3:16 expresses this comprehensively, and Jesus himself told us that there is joy in heaven over *one* sinner who repents (Lk 15:10). Therefore my favourite hymn is the Spiritual "Oh when the saints go marching in" with the chorus "Let me be among that number." And when they crown him king of kings, I want to be present, and I want to invite as many as possible to be there as well.

3.3 The Church Came (and still Comes) after the Mission

Here I follow Martin Kähler,[5] who recognized and published that the New Testament was not the product of the early church but of the early mission, and that both the gospels and the New Testament letters were the result of that

---

[5] Martin Kähler (1835-1912) was Professor of Systematic Theology and New Testament at Halle University. For easy access to his writings see: Martin Kähler, *Schriften zu Christologie and Missiologie,* München, 1971. For his life see Wikipedia. Also: www.heiligenlexikon.de/BiographieM/Martin_Kähler.html.

mission.⁶ That shows the (temporal and substantial) priority of mission before the church.⁷ It also reminds us that Jesus chose, as his successors, twelve *missionaries* (*apostoloi*, sent ones), and not twelve Administrators or Bishops. I have nothing against bishops, as long as their office is seen as a useful result of a (church-) historical process and not as a dogmatic or biblical necessity.⁸

3.4 Missions are the Children of Revivals

That I learnt soon after my conversion (1955) when I started to read the German Protestant missions' magazines.⁹ That held equally true when I started to become a missiologist, and when I embarked on my study of the concept of the church in the Faith Missions, but I had to make a small change. It was no longer "Missions are the children of *the* Revival" but "Missions are the children of [*different*] revivals." In the 1950s most German Protestant missions were indeed children of one specific revival, the Great Awakening, which began in 1734 (Jonathan Edwards) and which gave birth in 1792 (William Carey) to the modern Protestant world mission. In my studies I observed that each new revival produced new missions, and I based my typology of the Protestant missions (since 1517) on the origins of the missions in the various revivals.¹⁰

3.5 Kenneth Scott Latourette

I am a proud student of this mission historian, who is perhaps the most important of them all.¹¹ His understanding is that the Holy Spirit moves forward the history of

---

6   That includes the Revelation, which is in much of its literary form an apocalypse, but was as well a missionary letter. The concluding message of the book is: "Whoever is thirsty, let him come; and whoever wishes, let him take the free gift of the water of life" (Rev 22:17).

7   This makes me extremely critical of all attempts to "integrate mission(s) into the church" and equally so of the more recent idea of "the missional church." When everything is mission, nothing is mission anymore, and when everything in a church is "missional," there is no room for missions either. (I once attended a full length lecture on the "missional church" and heard nothing on missions in that hour.)

8   This means that I see no chance for (and no justification in) the ecumenical endeavour to achieve (greater) church unity by the mutual recognition of ecclesiastical office in the form of the "threefold office" (Deacon, Priest, Bishop) as promoted in the Lima Document.

9   These were the magazines of the "ecumenical" German missions in the late 1950s. These days such things are rarely mentioned.

10 Klaus Fiedler, "Die Vielfalt der evangelischen Missionsbewegung – Der Versuch einer historischen Typologie", in: *Evangelikale Missiologie* 7 (1992), pp. 80-82.

11 His importance is, of course debated. But he wrote the most comprehensive history of world missions, and several reprints were well justified.

the church by bringing in ever new revivals that produce ever new organizations. Latourette emphasizes, appropriately for a church historian, that it is the Holy Spirit who moves forward church history. For Latourette revivals can not be produced, but he observes that they do recur again and again, though there is no timetable for that which we may be able to read.

Such revivals bring large numbers of people to a personal faith in Christ,[12] and such a new won faith they translate into action, regularly expressed in founding new organizations.[13] Such organizations range from Bible societies to societies for prison reform, from associations to fight the slave trade to missions at home and abroad. In his systematic treatment of the issue, Latourette does not talk of new denominations as children of the revivals, but in his historical presentation they are clearly seen as products of the revivals. If new *churches* (denominations) can be children of revivals, then Christian pluralism can not be evil in principle. Then they are not an expression of the badly *divided* body of Christ, but they are expressions of the vitality of the *one* body of Christ.[14] The foreign missions are for Latourette the most important result of the revivals as they were important tools for the expansion of the Christian faith.[15]

3.6 Missiology and other Fields of Theology

I am convinced that missions must be in the centre. Where does that leave Biblical or Systematic Theology? They have their places, and very important places indeed. But always with one provision: They must point to the centre, to faith in Christ and to conversion to Christ for those who do not yet know him.

---

[12] They suddenly understand that the sacraments they all have received do not make them Christians at all. (That was even the message of Ludwig Doll, minister of the established [folk-] church and the founder of Neukirchen Mission, the first German Faith Mission. For its history see Bernd Brandl, Die Geschichte der Neukirchener Mission als erste deutsche Glaubensmission, PhD, ETF Leuven, 1997, published as: Bernd Brandl, *Die Neukirchener Mission. Ihre Geschichte als erste deutsche Glaubensmission*, Köln: Rheinland Verlag; Neukirchen-Vluyn, Verlag des Erziehungsvereins, 1998.)

[13] That disturbs the feelings of all who believe that the Christian faith finds its highest fulfillment if the church is organized into as few denominations as possible.

[14] See Klaus Fiedler, "Unity does not Promote Missions. The Case for Christian Diversity in Malawi (and maybe elsewhere)," to be published.

[15] For Latourette geographical expansion of the worldwide church is a major criterion for the vitality of the church at any given time, besides "new movements" and the "effects of Christianity" (Kenneth Scott Latourette, *A History of Christianity*, vol 1 to AD 1500, Peabody: Prince Press, [7]2007, p. xxi).

3.7 Modalities – Sodalities

I do not like this terminology, but since it comes from America it must be good enough even for us. Anyhow, it expresses an important theological truth: The church of Jesus Christ is not just the organized and well structured church (modality), but the church is equally so the organizations and structures born from the faith of the [revival] Christians (sodalities). According to Latourette, and here I fully agree, what moves forward church history are the sodalities.[16]

In the missiology of the Gustav Warneck School the mission societies were seen as the (effective) agents to implement the missionary task which the (organized) churches had neglected so efficiently. Contrary to Warneck I do not see the sodalities as a substitution for the churches, but I see them as being fully the church, not its only expression, but a genuine and independent expression of the church.[17]

Here in Malawi this means that I teach my students in Missiology that Africa was not evangelized by the European and American *churches* but by the *mission societies* from Europe and America, and those came from the various revivals.[18] And what is true for Africa is true for the rest of the world.[19] The well organized churches (the modalities) contributed little to the evangelization of the non-Christian world.[20]

---

[16] Latourette lived before the term was invented. He speaks of organizations produced by the revival. He emphasizes again and again the role of the religious orders, attracting and reflecting the dedication and commitment of many who are enthusiastic about following Christ.

[17] If the missions are church (and what else could they have been?), the "Integration of the missions into the church" as propagated in New Delhi 1961 makes no sense.

[18] The picture I draw here is Protestant. The (organized) Roman Catholic Church was more directly involved in missions, but even in the Catholic Church the bulk of the foreign missionary work was done by the religious orders (sodalities like with the Protestants). Many of them like the White Fathers and the White Sisters come from the Catholic counterpart of the Great Awakening or were motivated by it for foreign missions (like the Montfort Fathers and the Ladies of Wisdom).

[19] "Few in ecclesiastical leadership had the remotest idea that the so often struggling [missionary] movement was to be instrumental in the transformation of the demographic and cultural composition of the Christian church. A movement that arose in the heart of Christendom helped Christianity to survive the death of Christendom." (Andrew F. Walls, *The Cross-Cultural Process in Christian History*, Edinburgh: T&T Clark; New York: Orbis, 2002, p. 235.)

[20] It was the Church Missionary Society (1799), which spread the Anglican Church across the world (in the early years often with German missionaries from the Great Awakening like

3.8 The Characteristics of Revivals

Revivals are very divers, and so are the organizations and structures they produce. Common to all of them is that almost all of them came into existence outside the structures outside the structures of the established churches and that they had no intention to establish new churches. Common to all of them is that through them people find a (personal) faith in Christ. Those revived get interested in reading the Bible, in Christian fellowship and in a life of holiness and service.[21] All revivals have the tendency to blur the existing distinctions between Jesus' disciples. They do not abolish these, but they reduce them. Four of these are the most important for me:

(1) The difference between **clergy** and **laity** is reduced. When revival comes, laymen are often the leaders or leading evangelists[22] and ordination loses some or much of its importance.[23]

Krapf and Rebmann [Steven Paas, *Johannes Rebmann. A Servant of God in Africa before the Rise of Western Colonialism*, Bonn: VKW, Nürnberg: VTR, 2011]), with the modality, the Church of England, making her contribution by ordaining the bishops (considered necessary for Anglicans). (I simplify a bit here, and the Society for the Propagation of the Gospel also must not be overlooked.) – That is true even today. Though all the major Protestant churches have a mission department, most of their money is spent on interchurch aid and charity (call it development aid), not as a means to convert the heathen as William Carey proposed in 1792.

[21] That is how Mark van Koevering (Anglican Bishop of Niassa, Mozambique) described the revival in his diocese, in whose origins Fanuel Magangani participated, now his neighbour as the Bishop of Northern Malawi.

[22] Here in Malawi during the revival of the 1970s important leaders were Shadrack Wame (gardener) and Andrew Gabriel (tailor). See Bright Kawamba, The Blantyre Revival of the 1970s, MA, University of Malawi, 2013. For Shadrack Wame see also: Ernst Wendland, *Preaching that Grabs the Heart. A Rhetorical-Stylistic Study of the Chichewa Revival Sermons of Shadrack Wame*, Blantyre: CLAIM-Kachere, 2000.

[23] Grattan Guinness, Dwight Lyman Moody and Charles Haddon Spurgeon, all important leaders of the Evangelical Revival (Holiness Revival, Second Evangelical Awakening) were never ordained and never realized that they had missed something. And if we count the fruits of their labours as evidence, they were as much endowed with the Holy Spirit as their properly ordained colleagues. Thomas Spurgeon, Evangelist and Pastor of the Tabernacle Baptist Church in Auckland, of which Joseph Booth, the first faith missionary in Malawi was once a member, opined that the Australian Steamship Company had ordained him by granting him for his journey to Tasmania the reduced minister's rate. (Klaus Fiedler, *The Making of a Maverick Missionary. Joseph Booth in Australasia*, Zomba: Kachere, 2006. See also the section: "Ordination of the Pierced Hands" in Klaus Fiedler, *The Story of Faith Missions from Hudson Taylor to Present Day Africa*", Oxford et al: Regnum, 1994, pp. 186-187.)

(2) The difference between **women** and **men** is reduced. When revival comes, women forget that they really should be quiet in the church, looking after the children and the kitchen, and they become preachers (Catherine Booth), teachers of holiness (Phoebe Palmer), organizers of healing homes (Mrs Baxter), evangelists (Nellie Hall), missionaries (Malla Moe, Swaziland; Bessie Fricker, Guinea Bissau) or even pastors (Free Methodists, USA).[24]

(3) The **social differences** (class, race, nationality) lose much of their defining power. When revival comes, the rich landowner prays with his workers,[25] black Kenyans refuse to dissociate themselves from their white brethren even in the days of Mau Mau, the wealthy Parliamentarian Wilberforce decides to live a simple life fighting against the slave trade specifically and against slavery in general, and the first Moravian missionary marries a coloured woman,[26] and the Faith Missions consider themselves all as being international.[27]

(4) The differences between **denominations** get blurred. This does not happen through a process of gradual rapprochement (convergence),[28] nor through negotiations between churches (church union,[29] uniting churches, organic unity, reconciled diversity), but through emphasis on personal faith in Jesus Christ, blissfully ignoring a good number of ecclesiastical doctrines and the confessions that support them.[30] This

---

[24] Klaus Fiedler, *The Story of Faith Missions from Hudson Taylor to Present Day Africa*, Oxford et al: Regnum, 1994, pp. 292ff. "Using (no longer) neglected forces."

[25] An example from Germany are the von Bülows in Pommerania (Gottfried Sommer, Die 'Belowianer' in Hinterpommern. Ihr Weg vom enthusiastischen Aufbruch zur Bildung einer Freikirche, PhD, Evangelical Theological Faculty Leuven, 2010.)

[26] For that he and his wife and the colleague who married them were accommodated in the prison of the Danish colony of St Thomas. When Nikolaus Count of Zinzendorf (1700-1760) went there to see how they were (he had received no mail for a year), the Governor of the island was somewhat upset to have to collect them from prison, when the Count asked where his brothers were, and he was negatively impressed when the same Count greeted the coloured female prisoner by kissing her hand, a greeting reserved in those days for female members of the nobility. But was she not his sister?

[27] WEC International is so international that it moved its headquarters from Bulstrode (UK) to Singapore.

[28] That is the foundation of the Lima Process.

[29] Here the Church of South India is the shining example.

[30] This attitude found its expression in the "Basis" of the Evangelical Alliance (1856), which contains no ecclesiology arguing that, different from the issues of salvation, serious and

> makes the revivalist (and therefore the Evangelical) conception of Christian unity to be individual and not corporative as is the concept of unity of the churches with an ecumenical orientation.[31]

All revivals (at least since 1600) have one common message: You must be born again (conversion, personal faith). This message finds expression in various ways, different in form, but basically identical. In addition revivals tend to have a secondary message, typical for a specific revival.[32]

We are all convinced that revivals are God's great blessing. If we take that belief seriously, we must be willing to accept a lot of disorder and some outright chaos, because revivals challenge the organized church(es) in many ways, not only their habits and their (more or less well) organized structures, but also, and strongly so, their doctrine of the sacraments and the doctrine of church office that undergirds them.[33] Revivals do not only disturb the folk-churches, but they have that capacity

---

honest readers of the New Testament may reach different conclusions. – Such ignoring of the ecclesiastical tradition found its extreme expression in the Restorationist Revival (1812), which postulated that it is possible to leave all ecclesiastical traditions aside and to find direct access to the New Testament (and that would also create the unity of all believers). The history of the churches born in the Restorationist Revival (Churches of Christ/Christian Churches/Disciples, Christian Brethren and the Catholic Apostolic Church shows that this is not possible. Instead of reducing Christian diversity, they increased it measurably (Klaus Fiedler, "A Revival Disregarded and Disliked" [A proposal to recognize the Restorationist Revival in the Writing of Mission and Church History] in Klaus W. Müller (ed.), *Mission in fremden Kulturen*. Edition afem, mission academics, vol. 15, Nürnberg: VTR, 2003).

[31] These different concepts of unity found their expression in the (Ecumenical) World Council of Churches and in the (Evangelical) Lausanne Movement, which held its third big conference in Cape Town in 2010.

[32] For the Evangelical Revival (1858) it was the message of Power for Service, transmitted in a specific holiness/sanctification experience (Keswick style). Later some added the message of the soon return of Christ (prämillennial). On the role of the expectation of the imminent return of Christ for the Faith Missions see: Klaus Fiedler, *Ganz auf Vertrauen. Geschichte and Kirchenverständnis der Glaubensmissionen*, Giessen/Basel: Brunnen, 1992 (Chapter on the Prophetic Movement). The book is available for free download: http://tinyurl.com/fiedler.

[33] For a church organized on sacramental lines it is difficult to swallow when the revival people (most of them not even a little bit ordained) insist that baptism (even if followed by confirmation) does not produce salvation. – In Edinburgh 1910 the doctrine of the sacraments was the determining conflict with the Evangelicals.

also for the evangelical churches.³⁴ Another disturbing element is that revivals have the capacity to develop extreme branches, some of which are even difficult to still recognize as being Christian.³⁵

When we study revivals, we must note that revivals are not just born and flourish ever after, but they also decline and may even die. But even when they decline, they usually leave an important inheritance: institutions, fellowship movements, mission societies and theological insights.

Of course, such an inheritance is prone to change as time goes on, but often the core values are retained even after generations. On the other hand there are cases where institutions born in revival lose, together with the initial fervour, some or many of their original achievements, as it has been said of a number of the Classical Missions which were born in the Great Awakening.³⁶

4 The First 1600 Years

I am not a specialist for this period, so I can only mention a few things that seem obvious to me.³⁷

---

³⁴ When in 1906 the Pentecostal Movement defined the "full blessing of Pentecost" differently from the Holiness Movement, many Holiness people moved to the Pentecostals, but the Holiness Movement as a whole refused (Germany is a well known example, where the rejection was expressed in the Berlin Declaration of 1910, only recently set aside by mutual agreement). The Christian and Missionary Alliance lost a third of their members to the Pentecostals, but as a whole did not join the movement, and neither did Alexander Dowie, the leading healing evangelist of that time. (But in South Africa his Catholic Apostolic Church merged with the Pentecostal Movement there. [Ulf Strohbehn, *The Zionist Churches in Malawi. History – Theology – Anthropology*, Mzuzu: Mzuni Press, 2015]).

³⁵ The Restorationist Revival gave birth to the New Apostolic Church (which currently refuses fellowship with all other Christians), the Jehovah's Witnesses (who do not consider themselves to be a church but see themselves as God's *Theocratic Organization*), and the Church of Jesus Christ of the Latter Day Saints ("Mormons"), who through additional holy books and polytheistic concepts have effectively denied their Christian origins (Klaus Fiedler, "'A Revival Disregarded and Disliked' or What do Seventh-day Adventists, Churches of Christ, Jehovah's Witnesses and the New Apostolic Church have in Common?" *Religion in Malawi* 15 (2009), pp. 10–19.

³⁶ A strong example for such loss of the original values is the World Students Christian Federation, born from the Student Volunteer Movement.

³⁷ Here again I am a student of Latourette.

4.1 The Sodalities

I am not a proponent of theories of the decline of the (original, "primitive") church,[38] but it can not be denied that around the end of the third Christian century, the church had developed in some cases along "folk-church" lines, so that the hermits decided to withdraw (from both the world and—in a way—the church) into the desert.[39] Pachom and his sister Mary started the first monasteries to give men and women the chance to withdraw from the world while still living in a community. These sodalities of monks and nuns, over the centuries, became probably the most powerful force in both Christian missions and Christian renewal.

In the Near East and in the Orthodox Churches monasticism found its basic expression in the rule of Basileos (330-379), and the missions into the interior of Asia were largely carried out by monks.[40]

In the Latin Christianity of Western Europe it was Benedict of Nursia (Monte Cassino, 547) who gave Western monasticism its lasting structure through his famous Rule. The conviction that prayer and work ("ora et labora") form a unity made them to be capable pioneer missionaries in remote parts (and in the Europe of those days there were plenty of those). Around the same time Irish monasticism developed its far reaching missionary activity, reaching right into the heartlands of Europe.[41] In this movement the power of the bishops was limited to ordination.[42]

That the religious orders were the children of revivals also shows in their decline and renewal (after shorter or longer periods). After a time the Holy Spirit would bring a new revival, as it happened through the founding of the monasteries

---

[38] The Plymouth Brethren dated the beginning of this decline very early, between Paul's first and second letter to Timothy, because Paul writes in 2 Tim 2,20: "In a large house there are articles not only of gold and silver, but also of wood and clay; some are for noble purposes and some for ignoble." The Churches of Christ dated the beginning decline after the New Testament was finished, and they called upon all Christians to go back to the point before the decline started. Even today Churches of Christ buildings sometimes carry the inscription: Founded 33 AD.

[39] That such withdrawal from society did not mean enmity shows St Anthony's support for Athanasius in the Arian controversies.

[40] A-lo-pen (we only know his Chinese name) founded the church in China through the establishment of a monastery, and there is some evidence that the Church of the East (often wrongly named Nestorians) even had two monasteries in Japan (which today still exist as Buddhist monasteries).

[41] Congregations of Bad Urach and Bad Liebenzell have Irish monks as their founders. St Gallen (Switzerland) and Bobbio (South Tyrol) are famous Irish foundations.

[42] This is also true of the Moravian Church.

of Cluny (909) and Citeaux (1097, Cistercians) and the spirituality that spread from there.

In the 13th century a new wave of revival swept through Latin Christianity that led to the formation of new religious sodalities like the Franciscans with their new understanding of the vow of poverty[43] and the Dominicans with their emphasis on preaching when that was not so common in the Catholic Church. St Francis, travelling with the crusaders opposing their spirit, tried to bring the Gospel to the Sultan in Egypt, and when the doors to the world opened, the Franciscans became a prominent missionary order.[44] St Dominic understood his missionary task as firstly directed toward the heretics, and it is said that through his happiness he convinced many of the Albigensians.[45] With the discovery of the new world, the Dominicans became a major missionary order as well.

Equally dedicated to the ideal of poverty was Peter Valdes. Like St Francis he heard the call: "Sell what you have and give it to the poor," and like the Franciscans he and the "Poor of Lyon" tried to live their calling as wanderers, and like St Dominic they tried to preach the gospel everywhere. But different from Francis and Dominic they received neither papal toleration nor approval.[46] They were great missionaries in many parts of Western and Central Europe, but through brutal persecutions by the Roman Catholic Church and by governments supporting it, they were pushed back into a few of the Alpine valleys.

4.2 The Missions

When writing about the sodalities I have mentioned already several times their missionary activities. Since Christian (Latin) Europe was so hemmed in (through the Atlantic Ocean in the West, the Siberian wilderness in the North and the Muslim barrier in the South and the East), their foreign mission efforts remained limited in

---

[43] The Benedictines understood poverty as personal poverty, while St Francis and St Clara extended this poverty to the order itself, which were called mendicant orders. St Francis' piety was so contagious and so extreme that even during his lifetime the vow of poverty had to be "softened."

[44] For a discussion of the female aspects of that revival see: Frank Chirwa, A Critical Examination of the Changing Role of Women in the Seventh-day Adventist Church in Malawi: A Historical, Theological and Socio-Cultural Analysis, PhD, Mzuzu University, 2014 ("Women during the Vita Apostolici Restorationist Revival 12th-13th Century), pp. 117ff.

[45] His missionary method markedly differed from that of the French king who evangelized the Albigensians (with the approval of Pope Innocent III) through several crusades (1208-1250) against which the crusades in the Holy Land were comparatively harmless.

[46] That they could not retain the papal blessing may have been due to the fact that the "Poor of Lyon" placed the Bible in the hands of the lay people (typical for revivals).

the early years. St Francis had tried to convert the Muslim Sultan, but though he was received well, the Sultan did not accept the Gospel. That encounter did not lead to the founding of a mission among Muslims. There was only one opening, and that was into Inner Asia. The Franciscan missionaries followed that opportunity, and travelled on the silk road to China, where they started the Archbishopric of Beijing.[47]

The Dominicans saw Mission first of all as the conversion of the heretics.[48] What Dominic promoted through his smile, was later done by the Inquisition, an indication as to what can go wrong with a revival.

The Valdensians (as a sodality) were very missionary, but the Church (as a modality) denied them not only life but also the space for missions.

5. The Reformations

Latourette dates the second recession from 1350 to 1500.[49] This recession saw the loss of large mission territories in Asia and a big loss of Christian commitment in Western Europe.[50]

The next revival, at least in its emerging Protestant form, did not come from the religious orders, but in conflict to them. It also came from territories which, in the centuries before, had contributed little to revivals (Germany, Switzerland, the Netherlands, England and Scotland). Of the four Protestant reformations[51] only the Anabaptist Reformation really had a missionary spirit,[52] but that was severely

---

[47] John of Montecorvino was the first Catholic missionary in China (1294). See Kenneth Scott Latourette, *A History of Christianity. Beginnings to* 1500, Peabody: Prince Press, ⁷2007 [San Francisco: Harper, 1953], p. 403.

[48] The Albigensians (Katharoi) may also be seen as a revival movement gone wrong, because, in their sincerity to be pure, they adopted some dualist ("Gnostic") teachings which were not really compatible with the Christian faith.

[49] Kenneth Scott Latourette, *A History of Christianity*, vol 1, Peabody: Prince Press, 2007 (1953, 1975), pp. 601-684.

[50] Here the Renaissance plays a role, as it had the tendency to place man in the centre of the universe and God at its fringe. Most of the Renaissance popes were famous for their love of the arts and of power and for their poor morals. When in 1492 Columbus discovered the new world ("India"), the church went with him, and there is some evidence that Columbus, as a member of a tertiary order, considered himself to have a missionary task.

[51] Lutheran (1517), Reformed/Presbyterian (1525), Anabaptist (1527), Anglican (1534), and Catholic (1545).

[52] George W. Peters, himself from the Mennonite Brethren and the one who proposed the establishment of the Association of German Speaking Evangelical Missiologists (AfeM),

hampered by multiple persecutions. I do not doubt that the other three Protestant reformations were major revivals, but in terms of foreign missions they had little to offer.

The Catholic Reformation was very different.[53] Here the religious orders (with the Jesuits in the lead) devoted themselves to the worldwide missionary task. All seven founder members of the Jesuits vowed to become missionaries. Only one of them managed, but with Francis Xavier (1506-1552) the Jesuits gave to Christianity one of its most successful and most famous missionaries. In the Spanish and Portuguese colonies there were a considerable number of secular priests, but the missionary advance into unevangelized territories was mostly carried out by the religious orders, which, with a sacrificial spirit[54] and often innovative methods, tried to reach the unreached.[55]

6 Pietists, Puritans and Orthodox Theologians

While the (Protestant) Reformers, at least in their theology, approved foreign missions,[56] their successors, the orthodox theologians, denied both the duty and

---

emphasized this very much. For the Anabaptists see: Kenneth Scott Latourette, A History of Christianity, pp. 778-787.

[53] I have problems in dating the Catholic Reformation. Contarini (later Cardinal) experienced his conversion (along similar lines as Martin Luther) in 1511. In 1517 the Oratory of Divine Love was founded in Rome (one of their innovative methods of evangelization were stage plays and the music of Palestrina), in 1522 Ignatius of Loyola found Christ, and the first Reform Pope Paul III (1534-1549) in 1545 called for the Council of Trent (1545-1547, 1551-1552, 1562-1563), and in 1536 Teresa of Avila became a Carmelite nun. – For a good overview see: Robert D. Linder, "The Catholic Reformation" in: Tim Dowley (ed), *The History of Christianity. A Lion Handbook*, Oxford, Batavia, Sydney: Lion, 1990, pp. 410-428.

[54] The Jesuits count more than a 1000 Martyrs in their history, most of them in the missions.

[55] Here the "Reductions" of the Jesuits were a shining example. They attracted tens of thousands of Indians to give up their nomadic lifestyle in the Chaco and to live with them. In Paraguay the Reductions fell victim to anti-Jesuit efforts in Europe. In California the Jesuit missions were destroyed by the secularist policies of the Mexican government, so that the "liberation" of the Californian Indians meant their destruction.

[56] Calvin approved the attempt of some French Protestants to settle in South America, but he seems not to have been too much troubled (in his theology) when, having failed, they returned and reported that the Indians there obviously had heard the Gospel from the apostles (who had come there by divine transport) and had rejected it, for themselves and their descendants over all the generations (Letter from Peter Richter to Calvin, 31.3.1557, in

the right to evangelize the world, and the universities of Wittenberg[57] and Tübingen duly produced the required theological statements. Their aim was to defend biblical truth (or what they saw as such).[58] Anti-Catholic as they were, they could not see the Pope as the successor of the apostles. To make sure about that, they limited the biblical office of apostle to the Twelve.[59] Equally they limited the Great Commission to them, arguing that it was given to the twelve apostles personally (*ad personam*). And, of course, they carried out what they had been commanded, literally and enthusiastically, but unfortunately some of the nations they evangelized rejected the message for themselves and even for their

---

Werner Raupp, *Mission in Quellentexten. Von der Reformation bis zur Weltmissionskonferenz 1910*, Erlangen/Bad Liebenzell: Verlag der Evang.-Luth. Mission/Verlag der Liebenzeller Mission, 1990, p. 34. – Luther first wrote a book to invite the Jews to the Gospel (*Daß Jesus Christus ein geborener Jude sei*, 1523), then one about "the Jews and their Lies" (*Von den Juden und ihren Lügen*, 1543), which, so I am sure, had no positive missionary effect on the Jews.

[57] "Hierauf antworten wir (1.), daß solcher Befehl, ite in mundum universum, was die Freiheit betrifft, ohne ferneren Beruf [ohne fernere Berufung] an allen Orten und in der ganzen Welt zu lehren, allein die lieben Apostel und Jünger des HErren Christi angehe ... welchem Befehl sie dann auch gehorsam waren und treulich nachgekommen sind, [und] sind ausgegangen in alle Welt und haben an allen Orten geprediget (Marc. 16 V. 20) ... Es war aber dieses, wie auch die anderen Wundergaben ein personale privilegium [persönliches Vorrecht], so die Successores [Nachfolger] nicht erben, sonst müßten kraft solchen Befehls alle und jeder Prediger selbst in alle Welt ausgehen und predigten, welches gleichwohl nicht geschieht ... sondern ein jeder ist schuldig bei seiner Kirche zu bleiben, dahin er ordentlicherweise berufen worden ist." (To this question we answer (1.) that such a command to go into all the world, without a special calling, to teach at any place and all over the world, concerned only the dear Apostles and the Disciples of the Lord Christ ... and they did obey that command and carried it out faithfully. They went into all the world and preached everywhere (Mk 16:20) ... But this command, as much as the gift to perform miracles, was given as a *personal privilege*, not to be passed on to their successors, otherwise each and every preacher would have to go into all the world to preach, which indeed is not happening ... therefore every pastor is obliged to stay with that church to which he has been called." (*Consilia theologica Witebergensia, Das ist Wittenbergische Geistliche Rathschläge deß theuren Mannes Gottes D. Martini Lutheri, seiner Collegen und treuen Nachfolger*, Frankfurt 1664, quoted in Werner Raupp, *Mission in Quellentexten. Von der Reformation bis zur Weltmissionskonferenz 1910*, Erlangen/Bad Liebenzell: Verlag der Evang.-Luth. Mission/Verlag der Liebenzeller Mission, 1990, p. 70).

[58] After all they were *orthodox* theologians and therefore right.

[59] And somehow they managed to get Paul into that number as well.

descendants (of any number of generations).[60] And when the Twelve Apostles died (who, by definition, could have no successors),[61] the Great Commission was no longer valid.[62] Anyone wanting to be a missionary after the death of the last of the (twelve) apostles, would make himself to be an apostle, and that must not happen on any account, anti-Catholic as one is. If one wants to alleviate the orthodox theologians' enmity to foreign missions a little, one may point out that they indeed forbade foreign missions, but also taught that Christian princes, who acquire heathen territories, are obliged to establish churches there, and these must allow access to all comers.[63]

After missions had been declared as being sin, the revivalists preferred not to follow the theology of the universities. In America this led to the missionary work of David Brainerd and John Elliot among the Native Americans ("Red Indians").[64] In Germany it was the Moravians who successfully ignored the theology of the universities and who, starting in 1732, became the most successful missionary enterprise of those decades.[65] In Africa there were two Moravian missionary

---

[60] And if you ask, how they got to Australia or America, continents they knew nothing about, better question your faith: If God managed to transport Phillip to Asdod, why should larger distances be a problem for Him?

[61] Conservative Presbyterian theology even today defines apostles and prophets as "extraordinary officers of the church," incumbents of an office that does not exist any more.

[62] After all, they had effectively fulfilled it!

[63] The Danish-Halle Mission worked on this basis. The Danish king with his Pietist leanings could not find any volunteer among the Danish Lutheran pastors, so he asked the revival people in Halle, and August Hermann Francke (1692 in Halle), a Pietist ever ready for innovations, (orphanage, pharmacy, one of the best schools of his time, educating the poor with the rich), found the first two (and many other) missionaries for the Danish trade colony in Tranquebar, until the Enlightenment improved the academic achievements of the mission and ended its life.

[64] Because of the rapid advance of the white newcomers towards the West, nothing much has remained of these missions. But their diaries still remain a challenge for missions.

[65] The revival made many things possible: that the Count prayed with the craftsmen, and that he, as a nobleman, took the examination for Lutheran pastors (in Rostock in disguise, because noblemen were not supposed to be theologians). Although the Lutheran authorities found him to be sound in doctrine, the Moravians were free to accept either the Lutheran or the Reformed confessions (and as revivalists they had no problems with the differences between them). For Zinzendorf see Stefan Hirzel, *Der Graf und die Brüder*, Stuttgart: Quell, 1980; Wilhelm Faix, *Zinzendorf – Glaube und Identität eines Querdenkers*, Marburg: Francke, 2012.

attempt in the 18th century.⁶⁶ That at the Cape was terminated because the Dutch Reformed Church there (the modality) considered the ordination of the first Moravian missionary as invalid,⁶⁷ and that at Christiansborg, the Danish possession in Ghana, was abandoned after the death of almost all missionaries.⁶⁸

In the Netherlands representatives of the Nadere Reformatie,⁶⁹ related to Pietism in Germany and to Puritanism in England,⁷⁰ promoted foreign missions.⁷¹

While the Protestants were represented in world missions just by a few revival people, the Catholic Church, through its sodalities, pushed ahead into ever new territories, and that led to a decline of the Protestant share in world Christianity.⁷²

7 The Enlightenment

When the Great Awakening came, everything changed. The Enlightenment (Latourette's third recession) had put man as a rational being in the centre of the universe, and the theologians, who were influenced by Rationalism, could win

---

[66] Georg Schmidt, 1737, in Baviaanskloof (Genadendal). See "The Moravian Mission and the Moravian Church in Southern Africa", www.safrika.org/moraven.html. For details see: H.C. Bredekamp, A.B.L Flegg and Plüdderman (eds), *The Genadendal Diaries,* vol 1, Bellville: University of the Western Cape, 1992.

[67] 1792 the Moravians finally came back and found the Christians there led by a woman, Magdalena Vehettge Tikhue.

[68] The Moravian Church sent nine missionaries (1737-1770), only the first (Christian Protten, son of a Ghanaian mother and a Danish father) survived for any length of time. His ministry was interspersed with lengthy sojourns in Denmark. He died in Ghana in 1769 (Elizabeth Isichei, *A History of Christianity in Africa from Antiquity to the Present*, London: SPCK, 1995, p. 60).

[69] This was a "further reformation of church, state and society in word and deed" (Hoffie Hofmeyr). It was that "movement within the Dutch Reformed Church during the 17th and 18th centuries which, in the absence of a living faith, made both the personal experience of faith and godliness matters of central importance" (Doc Blad NR, 1995, p. 108).

[70] Important were: Gisbertus Voetius (1589-1676), Johannes Hoornbeek (1617-1666), Anna Maria von Schurman, Essenius, Van Lodenstein, J. Tellinck. My colleague at the Evangelical Theological Faculty in Leuven, Hoffie Hofmeyr, specializes in the study of Hoornbeek.

[71] See Johannes Hoornbeek, *De conversione indorum et gentilium,* 1669.

[72] Some orthodox theologians even argued that the Catholics (whom they did not like much otherwise) were so active in missions that the Protestants did not need to do it (Werner Raupp, *Mission in Quellentexten. Von der Reformation bis zur Weltmissionskonferenz 1910*, Erlangen/Bad Liebenzell: Verlag der Evang.-Luth. Mission/ Verlag der Liebenzeller Mission, 1990, p. 72-73).

neither the hearts nor the purses of their church members.[73] The Christian faith seemed to be on the way out, or maybe it could be preserved as a religion of good behaviour,[74] in which Jesus plays the role of the liberator from man's self imposed ignorance and where sanctification means to live a rational life.[75] Such rationalist theology could not produce foreign missions, and it successfully brought to an end the Danish-Halle Mission in Tranquebar,[76] which (irrational) Pietism had created.[77] One may express it thus (of course, a bit simplified): A theology that removes Jesus from the centre does not produce any missions.

8 The Great Awakening

And then the revival came, unplanned and unexpected. It is called the Great Awakening not only because millions were converted to Christ, but also because it gave church history (and in many aspects even world history) a new direction and dramatically changed the religious geography of the world.

8.1 The Awakening

The awakening erupted in 1734, when Jonathan Edwards preached the (thoroughly non-rationalistic) sermon: "The Sinner in the Hands of an Angry God." Of course, even before that Jonathan Edwards had preached about the seriousness of sin and about the divine offer of forgiveness, but that had started no revival. (It seems that it is the Holy Spirit that brings revival according to his own timetable and

---

[73] This can be understood when we read that one of the rationalist pastors (who was so kind as to have his sermons printed) preached on Palm Sunday against the evil habit of wantonly cutting trees and on Easter about the blessing of getting up early, because the women had gotten up early and met Jesus.

[74] Frederic the Great and his friend Voltaire were convinced of the usefulness of the church for bringing up the children and for the moral improvement of the ordinary folk.

[75] "Enlightenment means going out of self-imposed ignorance."

[76] For the Tranquebar Mission see: Hans-Werner Gensichen, "Dänisch-hallische Mission", in Gerhard Krause and Gerhard Müller (eds), *Theologische Realenzyclopädie*, vol 7, Berlin/New York 1981, pp. 319-322; Arno Lehmann, *Es begann in Tranquebar – Die Geschichte der ersten Evangelischen Kirche in Indien*, Berlin, ²1956; Julius Richter, "Die Dänisch-Hallesche Mission in ihrer Bedeutung für die evangelische Missionsgeschichte," *Allgemeine Missionszeitschrift*, 1906, pp. 301-318.

[77] Even Liberal theology, in many ways heir to Rationalist theology, was not engaged in foreign missions. The only attempt was the Deutsche Ostasienmission, but after a time it gave up its liberal theology and became one of the Classical Missions.

geography.)[78] Since 1734 all worldwide revivals started in America, which is a sign of God's grace.[79] All these revivals tend to cross quickly the Atlantic and any other oceans. In England it was John Wesley, whose life was dramatically changed by the Great Awakening.[80] His brother Charles soon went the same way, and we should not forget George Whitefield, who became so important for America; both, like John Wesley, became great evangelists.

Revivals are always innovative.[81] The Pietists invented the home cell,[82] the Moravians organized their congregation into choirs (not for singing), and John Wesley, not only a great evangelist but also a great organizer, was convinced that every new convert needed a spiritual home and so he organized the Methodist societies.[83]

---

[78] For a good overview see: A. Skevington Wood, "Awakening" in: Tim Dowley (ed), *The History of Christianity. A Lion Handbook*, Oxford, Batavia, Sydney: Lion, 1990, pp. 436-452 and in the same book "The Methodists", pp. 453-457.

[79] In spite of this America is unlikely the nation elected by God to rule the world.

[80] This has happened when he attended "rather unwillingly" on 24.5.1738 a Moravian home cell in Aldersgate, where, while Martin Luther's introduction to the Letter to the Romans was read, his heart was "strangely warmed." In Germany people often speak of this event as Wesley's conversion, but I prefer to speak of a second blessing or holiness experience, because he was a [real] Christian even before attending that home cell meeting. —Wesley's own words from his journal describing the experience were: "In the Evening I went very unwillingly to a Society in Aldersgate Street, where one was reading Luther's Preface to the Epistle to the Romans. About a Quarter before nine. While he was describing the Change which God works in the Heart thro' faith in Christ, I felt my heart strangely warm'd. I felt I did trust in Christ, Christ alone for Salvation: And an Assurance was given me, That He had taken away my Sins, even mine, and saved me from the Law of Sin and Death."

[81] This seems to be contradicted by the observation that the pious people seem to be rather conservative (or backward, to use a less friendly term). But these people were very innovative in those days when the revival was still young!

[82] Philipp Jakob Spener (1635-1705) called it ecclesiola in ecclesia, which he introduced in Frankfurt, where he was the leading pastor in the city. In 1675 he formulated his programme in the book *Pia Desideria*. (Philip Jacob Spener, *Pia Desideria*, trans. Theodore G. Tappert, Philadelphia: Fortress, 1964). For a scholarly study of Spener see: Johannes Wallmann, *Philipp Jakob Spener und die Anfänge des Pietismus*, 1970. For a quick overview of his life see Wikipedia.

[83] These Societies were, typical for revivals, independent from the parishes, to which their member belonged ("by regulation"). Typical for such "fellowships", they were often led by the laity, were interdenominational, and women and men were members. Even though all members individually may attend the Sunday service of their denomination and partake equally regularly in that denomination's sacraments and sacramentals, their spiritual heart

As usual with the revival people, he and his colleagues were not interested in starting a new church. And, as it is usual with the revival people, he had no objections in case such a thing might happen. Missions were his highest aim and purpose, and when the Methodists in America began to spread, but were lacking the properly ordained (Anglican) pastors, he just ordained a few.[84] So the Methodists in the USA became a new church even during Wesley's lifetime while it happened in England only after his death. Because of this the Methodists could become very successful in evangelizing the ever further westwards moving frontier[85] and later in the evangelization of the slaves and then the black Americans.[86] The Anglicans were not innovative, so they lost the "frontier", which the (revivalist) Methodists and the equally revivalist Baptists gained.[87] Would it have been better, for the sake of Christian unity, for the Methodists to have waited for the Bishop of London to slowly establish the necessary church infrastructure? For them missions had priority, and in the Bible we do not read that the angels in heaven rejoice over a (male) man being ordained but over a sinner (male or female) who repents. For this reason missions must have priority over (even ecclesiastical) office.[88]

The Great Awakening also brought, typical for revivals, new opportunities for women. The Countess of Huntingdon evangelized not only her friends in the nobility, she also used her right as a countess to employ chaplains, to evangelize in

---

will beat much faster and more happily when they are attending the fellowship. This is why such fellowships have the possibility (not necessity) to develop into new churches.

[84] Wesley believed that ordination is a necessity for the administration of the sacraments. As the Anglican Church was not willing or not able to ordain the Methodist preachers in America, Wesley, himself an Anglican priest, broke the fundamental Anglican law that only a bishop in the apostolic succession may ordain. For him missions were more important than (Anglican) canon law.

[85] The invention of the Circuit Riders was very appropriate for the frontier, as horses and bibles were readily available, unlike properly organized parishes.

[86] Albert Raboteau, *Slave Religion. The „Invisible Institution" in the Antebellum South*, New York: OUP, 1978, see esp. 30-136, 143-145, 175, 207.

[87] I like the Spiritual that reflects the situation: "Baptists go by water, Methodists go by land, but before they go to heaven, they have to go hand in hand."

[88] The priority of the ecclesiastical office got the first Moravian missionaries on St Thomas into prison and robbed the new Christian church at Baviaanskloof (Genadendal) of their shepherd. His work was carried on by Magdalena Vehettge Tikhue for over 40 years, until the Moravian missionaries returned (J.A. Millard, "Tikhuie, Vehettge Magdalena", www.dacb.org/stories/southafrica/tikhuie_vmagdalena.html).

many parts of Britain.[89] In the Methodist societies right from the beginning women played a major role, some developed into leaders and evangelists, and one of them received from Wesley even the Preacher's Certificate, giving her the highest rank available among Methodists at that time.[90]

The Great Awakening did not only produce the Methodists, but gave also new life to the Anglican Church (and other churches),[91] which gave birth to the Evangelical Party in the Church of England.[92]

The Great Awakening reached Scotland, among others through Jonathan Edwards' writings, which, also in England, led to a movement of concerted prayer.[93]

The Great Awakening was not only a new spiritual beginning for the churches, the Great Awakening also promoted all kinds of social improvements, from (urgently needed) prison reform to the (equally urgent) fight against poverty and disease,[94] from the repatriation of black Americans to Africa (in which they met

---

[89] For a time even George Whitefield was one of her chaplains. Later she was forced to declare her "chaplaincies" to be a denomination, the [Methodist] Huntingdon Connexion.

[90] See Paul Wesley Chilcote, *John Wesley and the Women Preachers of Early Methodism*, PhD, Duke University, 1984 (UMI). – Once Wesley had died, such things did not happen again for some time. When the Revival stabilizes (or declines), innovations become less.

[91] Of interest is here the case of the Baptists in England. They were the children of the Pietist/Puritan Awakening (1609). After the persecutions had reduced, many of them became liberal (of the Unitarian variant). Eight coal miners were saved in Methodist meetings, but felt that believers' baptism was more scriptural, so they approached the next Baptist church. That was a Particular Baptist church, so they could not baptize the eight Methodists, since they were Arminian in theology, but they were kind enough to tell the eight baptismal candidates that there was a General Baptist church in the same town that would accept them for baptism. That baptism brought the revival into the Baptist congregations and revived those that had not yet died. For a less anecdotal and more comprehensive version of the events see: John Briggs, "Early English Baptists" in: Tim Dowley (ed), *The History of Christianity. A Lion Handbook,* Oxford, Batavia, Sydney: Lion, 1990, pp. 406-409 [408].

[92] Charles Simeon (1759-1836) was the pioneer and leader of this group. See Oliver R. Barclay, *Simeon and the Evangelical Tradition,* np: Focus, 1988. See also www.satucket.com/lectionary/CharlesSimeon.htm.

[93] *A Humble Attempt to Promote Explicit Agreement and Visible Union of God's People in Extraordinary Prayer for the Revival of Religion and the Advancement of Christ's Kingdom on Earth, Pursuant to Scripture-promises and Prophecies Concerning the Last Time,* Boston 1747.

[94] My youngest daughter Katja was born in Florence Nightingale Hospital in Düsseldorf-Kaiserswerth, belonging to the Kaiserswerth Deaconesses, one of the women's movements

with little interest)[95] to the fight against first the slave trade and then slavery itself.[96]

8.2 The Missions

The revival was highly missionary from its beginning, but it took over 50 years until William Carey's efforts started Latourette's "Great Century" (1800-1914) of world missions.[97] Carey is a typical product of the revival: His conversion at the age of 14, his move from the Congregationalists to the Baptists,[98] that he became a pastor after four winters of primary school and without ever having been to a seminary, and that he had contacts to America and no qualms to contradict the current theology.[99]

---

of the Great Awakening, and my son Sascha has been working there as an anesthetic nurse for well over a decade.

[95] Here Sierra Leone (1787) was the first to receive such "returnees", which also led to the founding of the first Baptist church in Africa (Freetown). If the "returnees" still had a home in Africa is disputed. For Malawi Joseph Booth promoted the idea in his *Africa for the Africans*, and his success was close to zero.

[96] William Wilberforce (1759-1833), who led the struggle, had experienced a thorough conversion reading a Christian book (Philip Doddridge, *Rise and Progress of Religion in the Soul*) during an educational journey to the Continent 1784/5. – Non-Christian authors like Walter Rodney (*How Europe Underdeveloped Africa*, London/Dar es Salaam 1972) argue that the demise of slavery was caused by the (slowly growing) insight that slavery was no longer profitable. Maybe that was true, but Wilberforce and his friends needed much effort and quite a number of years to make the British business community aware of that.

[97] Kenneth Scott Latourette, *A History of the Expansion of Christianity*, vol. 7, *Advance through Storm*, Grand Rapids: Zondervan, ^{5}1976 (1945), 445, and vols 5 and 6 of his Mission History.

[98] In times of revival change of denomination is not a requirement but a frequent experience, because new spiritual experiences promote such change and because revival does not take doctrinal differentiations that seriously. Almost all founders of Faith Missions changed denominations at least once. An exception is Ludwig Doll (Neukirchen) who probably died too young for such a change.

[99] This is expressed in an anecdote that Elder Fuller, when Carey asked during a pastors' fraternal that the Christians' obligation to use means for the evangelization of the heathen, told him off with the words: "Sit down young man, if God wants to convert the heathen, he will do it without your help or mine". Physically the young man had to sit down, but spiritually he remained standing, and the topic was indeed discussed. It is quite possible that Elder Fuller never said these words, but if the story is invented, it is well invented as it reflects the then current theology of missions (or its opposite).

Equally typical for revivals, he was innovative. Though he was far too poor to buy books, he read them.[100] His interest was the whole world, quite a big view for a cobbler (but not so strange among the revivalists), he strongly promoted his education,[101] and didn't bow down before those in power. His most innovative (and most effective) idea was the missionary society. In his manifesto, the *Enquiry*,[102] he describes it:

> Suppose a company of serious Christians, ministers and private persons, were to form themselves into a society, and make a number of rules respecting the regulation of the plan, and the persons who are to be employed as missionaries, the means of defraying the expence, etc., etc. This society must consist of persons whose hearts are in the work, men of serious religion, and possessing a spirit of perseverance; there must be a determination not to admit any person who is not of this description, or to retain him longer than he answers to it.
>
> *From such a society a committee might be appointed*, whose business it should be to procure all the information they could upon the subject, to receive contributions, to inquire into the characters, tempers, abilities and religious views of the missionaries, and also to provide them with the necessaries for their undertakings.[103]

In 1792 and in the decades that followed, it was the *missionary societies* (and not the churches) that took upon themselves the task to evangelize the world. Andrew Walls points out that the Holy Spirit made a bit of fun of the churches (so well organized and so busy with themselves), set them aside and pursued his aims with those who were interested, willing and capable.[104]

---

[100] In the Map Room of the British Library I tried to find out, which of the contemporary atlases he had used as the base for the geographical section in his *Enquiry*. I think I checked them all, but could not find a single one that matched all of his geography, so I concluded that he had used mixed geographical sources. I published my reading of Carey's geography as: William Carey: *Eine Untersuchung über die Verpflichtung der Christen, Mittel einzusetzen für die Bekehrung der Heiden*. Translated and edited by Klaus Fiedler and Thomas Schirrmacher. With an English list of geographical identifications (edition afem – mission classics, vol. 1). Bonn: VKW, 1993; 2nd edition 1998.

[101] That he became Professor of Oriental Languages with a primary school education of four winters is an extreme case, but the revivalists regularly did much to improve their education and the education of their children. I have profited form that (my grandfather was a coal miner), Princeton University is a child of the Great Awakening, and the worldwide Seventh-day Adventist educational system equally has a revival base.

[102] William Carey, *An Enquiry into the Obligation of Christians to Use Means for the Conversion of the Heathens*, Leicester: Ann Ireland, 1792.

[103] Ibid., p. 82-83.

[104] Andrew Walls, "Vom Ursprung der Missionsgesellschaften – oder: Die glückliche Subversion der Kirchen," *Evangelikale Missiologie* 1987, 35-40; 56-60, after this published in English in *Evangelical Quarterly* 88:2 (1988), 141-155. – This article has been of special

William Carey and his friends translated the idea of the missionary society into reality.[105] They could not ask the bishops for permission, since the Baptists had none, but even the then Baptist authorities they did not ask for permission, but preferred to pay their bills themselves.[106] This attitude became typical for the new missionary movement. As is appropriate for the revival, the differences between ordained and lay were not given much importance[107] and women began to use much improved opportunities.[108] And the missionaries who then turned the religious world upside down, usually were ordained, but (equally usually) came from a social background[109] insufficient for a "proper" parson in England.[110]

---

importance to me. When I visited him in the course of my research into the ecclesiology of the Faith Missions, Professor Walls gave me the copy of a lecture he had once given. I liked it so much that I asked for permission to translate and publish it in *Evangelikale Missiologie*. He happily approved and that made him later publish the article even in English. Four years later it was him who gave me the hint that I might go to Malawi. I had visited him on the advice of Louise Pirouet, my first supervisor (who was also the one who convinced me to take mission history as my area of research) and to whom I dedicate this book.

[105] The Baptist Missionary Society was founded in 1792, for pedobaptist churches in 1795 the London Missionary Society was founded. Many other missions followed in America, in Great Britain, on the continent and in South Africa and Australasia.

[106] When revival comes there is always money.

[107] A good number of the early mission leaders were laymen, just as much as some of the pioneer missionaries like George Pilkington, famous for the Pilkington Revival of 1893 in Uganda. Others, though ordained, only had an "irregular" theological training, like Robert Moffat, the gardener, for six months with Rev Robert Caldwell (Bruce Ritchie, The Missionary Theology of Robert Moffat, PhD, University of Malawi, 2005, pp. 64-68.) Ritchie also traces carefully Moffat's revival roots.

[108] An outstanding example of such independent women was Mary Slessor, the "white queen" of Calabar. For an easily readable biography see: Basil Miller, *Mary Slessor. Heroine of Calabar*, Minneapolis: Bethany, 1974.

[109] Important pioneer missionaries in Southern Africa were Robert and Mary Moffat, working among the Tswana in Kuruman. Robert was a gardener and received a 6 months theological training. Mary was a teacher, whose parents, in the beginning, were reluctant to allow her to marry a man with lesser education. See Bruce Ritchie, The Theology of Robert Moffat of Kuruman, PhD, University of Malawi, 2006.

[110] In German classical missions there was the device of ordinations for the mission field, which lost their validity once the missionary returned to Germany. Since most of those who were willing to go abroad as missionaries did not have the qualification to study at a German University, Mission Seminars like Basel, Bethel, Neuendettelsau and Hermannsburg were founded.

The *Missions* of the Great Awakening changed the religious map of the world in dramatic ways. Without those missions the Protestant version of the Christian faith would have remained the folk religion of the (Western) Whites, and many areas of the world would never have been reached with the gospel (or much later in its Roman Catholic variety). The missions of the Great Awakening made a big contribution to the shift of the centre of Christian gravity southwards,[111] made black Africa to be dominant in the Anglican Community,[112] made the white Moravians to become a minority in their worldwide church[113] and created in Fourah Bay[114] in Sierra Leone the first University of black Africa.[115]

9 The Restorationist Interlude

When I wrote my book on the Faith Missions, I found that they were the typical missions of the Holiness Revival (the Evangelical Revival). In doing that I found that one of the roots of the Faith Missions was the Brethren Movement (Christian Brethren), which fit into none of the revivals I knew of.[116] Only here in Malawi did I realize that there were other revivalist movements at the same time, and that they

---

[111] According to the Edinburgh Atlas the Christian Centre of Gravity was in 1500 not far from Budapest, moved to Northern Italy in 1800, was found in 1910 in the Centre of Spain and in 2010 near Tessalit in Northern Mali, reflecting first the westward and then the southward trend of Christianity (Todd M. Johnson, Kenneth R. Ross, Sandra Lee (eds), *Atlas of Global Christianity 1910-2010*, Edinburgh University Press, 2009, p. 53.) The Anglican Centre of gravity moved from South Eastern France in 1910 to Northern Chad 100 years later. The Protestant Centre of gravity moved within the same period from North of the Azores into Northern Chad.

[112] If the spiritual centre also moved to Africa, maybe to Nigeria, Uganda or Rwanda, is a matter of debate depending on one's theological presuppositions. The email service "Virtuosity Digest" contains much information on this question. Of course, like all Information Services it is biased (and is honest enough not to hide this).

[113] In the Netherlands there are now 8 Moravian congregations, of these only Zeist is white, the others are black with their members mostly from a Surinamese ethnic background.

[114] When in 1876 Fourah Bay College affiliated with Durham University, some less then friendly contemporaries (in the satirical magazine *Punch*) proposed that Durham University should next affiliate with the London Zoo, grossly overestimating the animals' abilities.

[115] This is only true if the Islamic institutes of higher learning in Timbuktu are not counted as universities.

[116] See my Typology of the Protestant Missions in Klaus Fiedler, *Ganz auf Vertrauen*, Giessen/Basel: Brunnen, 1992 and http://tinyurl.com/fiedler. For the later English version see: Klaus Fiedler, *The Story of the Faith Missions*, Oxford: Regnum; Sutherland: Albatross, 1994.

all (besides evangelization) made the attempt to restore the "primitive church" and thereby restore the unity of the Christian denominations.[117] This approach had to fail not only because "Christianity so badly split" did not accept it, but because the New Testament does not show a clearly recognizable picture of the primitive church that could be implemented 1900 years later.[118]

When I did that research, I also observed that the second root of the Faith Missions was what I termed the "Prophetic Movement", whose oldest publication (to my knowledge) appeared in 1813, and which, over two generations, changed the predominant eschatology of the revival people from postmillennial to premillennial.[119] This Prophetic Movement had its strongest early exponents among the Christian Brethren (John Nelson Darby, George Müller) and in Irving (founder of the Apostolic Church),[120] and this caused me to extend the secondary message of the Restorationist Revival: "To restore the primitive church *once more before the end.*"[121]

For my topic it is important to realize that these movements, some of which look quite extreme to us, were revival movements. Their core message was conversion, they gave laymen new possibilities[122] and even women,[123] that they

---

[117] Because of this double emphasis I chose the name "Restorationist Revival".

[118] The Stone/Campbell Revival saw the New Testament Church as independent local churches led by elders; the Brethren saw the New Testament Church as the assembly of those gathered in biblical simplicity around the Lord's Table, the Apostolic Church (Edward Irving) saw the installation of twelve apostles (once before the return of Christ) and the regaining of the spiritual gifts as the necessary steps to restore the primitive church.

[119] There are exceptions: Most of the Churches of Christ did not accept premillennial eschatology.

[120] Of the original Apostolic Church there is a bare remnant left, but the New Apostolic Church has become a strong worldwide church. It seems to me that it is reducing its sectarian aspects.

[121] The Churches of Christ do not fit this extension of the definition fully, as they developed before the Evangelicals turned premillennial (and who, in their majority, rejected premillennialism), but it brought in the Seventh-day Adventists with their roots in the revival of William Miller (1782-1849) who saw it as their task as a remnant to call out of Christianity all those who were willing to prepare for the soon coming of Christ (but different from Miller [and from the Jehovah's Witnesses who come from a broadly related background] they did not date it). For more details see Stefan Höschele, *From the End of the World to the Ends of the Earth. The Development of Seventh-day Adventist Missiology,* Zomba: Kachere, 2004, pp. 13-20.

[122] The Brethren came to the conclusion that in the Church of the New Testament there were ministries, but no offices, and that therefore ordination was an unnecessary exercise. When the dentist Anthony Norris Groves, who was preparing for the [Anglican] ordination

used innovative ways and means of evangelism and they disturbed the Christian world quite a lot.

The Restorationist Revival differs from all other revivals in that it is interested in the church as an organized entity The ecclesiological disinterest of the other revivals made them jump easily from one denomination to the other(s) and probably revive them all, while the strong ecclesiological interest and its call for renewed Christian unity contributed a good number of new denominations to increase Christian diversity.

The Restorationist Revival also shows the danger of all revivals that the secondary message can take prime position, thus developing sectarian tendencies and reducing evangelism, often drastically,[124] and that liberal tendencies may produce the same results.[125]

---

understood this, he felt relieved and liberated. He then went to Baghdad (and later India) as the first of the many missionaries of the Open Brethren. (His biography is: Robert B. Dann, *Father of Faith Missions. The Life and Times of Anthony Norris Groves (1795-1853)*, Waynesboro: Authentic Media, 2004). As far as office and ordination are concerned, I feel at one with the Brethren. For over 10 years I was a member of the Brethren in Germany and Tanzania, and I have always understood my own ordination over 40 years ago at Hagen Baptist Church as a promise of (full time) ministry, but never as a necessity for it.

[123] This applies even to the Brethren and the Churches of Christ, who later told the women to shut up (Dan Been, *The Changing Role of Women in the Three Main Branches of the Stone/Campbell Restoration Movement*, Zomba: Kachere, 2011.)

[124] The Brethren split very early into an exclusive branch (John Nelson Darby) and an open branch (George Müller). The exclusive branch was prone to many splits, six up to 1900 alone. While the Open Brethren were very strong in world missions (in Africa especially in the "Beloved Strip" [North and East Congo, the Copperbelt, Northern Zambia and Northern Angola]), the foreign mission work of the Exclusive Brethren was minimal. In 1985 the Exclusive Brethren worldwide counted 171,668 members, the Open Brethren counted ten times as many (1,612,151) and in addition had made major contributions to other denominations, for example as missionaries of the China Inland Mission. Between 1970 and 1985 the Open Brethren grew by 28% and the Exclusive Brethren declined by 9% (*World Christian Encyclopedia*).

[125] This shows in the drastic decline of the membership of the Disciples, the liberal wing of the Stone/Campbell Movement in the USA, which emphasized the unity of all Christians and had, influenced by German Liberal Theology and based on Scottish Common Sense Philosophy developed a rationalistic interpretation of the Bible.

Regarding their somewhat limited numbers, the Restorationist Churches have made a considerable contribution to world missions.[126] They hardly developed their own missiology, though. The Brethren, more or less officially, joined the Evangelical camp,[127] the New Apostolic Church anyhow doesn't join anywhere, the Seventh-day Adventists remained somewhat alone due to their distinct theology, but though their missions sometimes found a place in ecumenical groupings, they developed a thoroughly Evangelical missiology.[128]

10 The Holiness Revival (Second Evangelical Awakening) and the Faith Missions

Because of their success on the mission fields and of declining enthusiasm at the home base, the advance of many of the Classical Missions slowed down or came to a halt around the second half of the 19th century. Though the Classical Missions of the Great Awakening had advanced much, their slow down left large areas of the world unreached: about a third of Africa (Sudan Belt, Congo Basin, Northern Africa),[129] all the interior of China (with more than 200 Million inhabitants), much of the Amazon and many "smaller" areas of the world.

---

[126] In Malawi the overall number of Restorationist Christians may be around a million (10% of the Christians). The Seventh-day Adventists with over 300,000 full members grow faster than average in spite or because of their strict rules (My student Macleard Banda sees both but emphasizes the "because". See Macleard Banda, "The Remnant and its Mission." An Investigation into the Interaction of the Seventh-day Adventist Church with Society in Malawi, PhD, Mzuzu University, 2014.)

[127] In Germany Forum Wiedenest (whose missionary I was for seven years in Tanzania, while it still carried the name Missionshaus Bibelschule Wiedenest) is one of the leading members of the Arbeitsgemeinschaft Evangelikaler Missionen (Association of Evangelical Missions). In Britain that is not possible, since the Christian Mission in Many Lands is still convinced that they are no mission society, but a simple organization to support individual missionaries commissioned by their individual local churches ("assemblies").

[128] Stephan Höschele, *From the End of the World to the Ends of the Earth. The Development of Seventh-day Adventist Missiology,* Zomba: Kachere, 2004.

[129] The report volume of the Edinburgh 1910 conference not only confirmed the fact that one third of it was still unreached, but also stated that no mission society had anything like a plan to enter that remaining third. That was largely true for the Classical Missions which were responsible for Edinburgh 1910 (though even here the efforts of the Church Missionary Society in Central Nigeria were being overlooked), but there was no reason to ignore the efforts made by the Faith Missions in that very area, starting in 1873 (Klaus Fiedler, "Edinburgh 2010 and the Evangelicals," *Evangelical Theological Review,* 34/4 (Oct 2010). pp. 53-71).

To reach China's Interior, Hudson and Maria Taylor[130] started in 1865 the China Inland Mission, not just another mission, but an innovative enterprise that wanted in no way compete with the Classical Missions (and hardly did so). The Taylors wanted, through the use of new spiritual resources (the piety of the Holiness Movement), with new personnel (converts of the Holiness Revival),[131] and new financial resources[132] to reach still unreached areas,[133] using innovative methods.[134]

For the China Inland Mission conversion had absolute priority (typical for Evangelicals). Therefore Hudson Taylor did not follow any specific ecclesiology (to those Anglicans who felt that bishops were a necessity, he gave their own province in West China,[135] while those who, like C.T. Studd, were not convinced of that necessity, served equally anywhere else.) And since evangelism was so urgent, Taylor emphasized the spiritual qualifications, though he did not despise theological studies.[136] So that more people could hear the Gospel, he gave equal

---

[130] To change denominations was typical for the founders of Faith Missions, and with Hudson Taylor especially so: Methodists – Free Methodists – Brethren – Mission Hall – Baptists.

[131] Most of the early China Inland Mission missionaries would have had no chance to be accepted by any of the Classical Missions. Joseph Booth, the first faith missionary to Malawi, applied to the Baptist Missionary Society, claiming that he wanted to implement the Industrial Missions approach first proposed by William Carey. But he had no chance there.

[132] With Hudson Taylor I do not believe that the available money for God's work is limited like a cake with a fixed size, so if there is a new mission it will take away the resources of other missions. Taylor was convinced that God had additional resources and that he would give them if the work is done as he wants it to be done ("God's work, done in God's way, will not lack God's supply"). As a historian I observe that God seems to make available such new resources predominantly through new revivals. Considering especially the early years of the Faith Missions, God obviously channeled some of the required resources from the Brethren, part of the Restorationist Revival.

[133] This was expressed in the name of the mission (China *Inland* Mission), and similarly in the names of many of the early Faith Missions: Livingstone Inland Mission, Africa Inland Mission, Sudan Interior Mission, Sudan Pionier Mission, Unevangelized Tribes Mission, Congo Inland Mission etc.

[134] Some of these were Itineration, tract distribution, wearing Chinese dress (including pig tail, until in 1910 China dropped it).

[135] There the CIM even produced an Anglican Bishop.

[136] He refused Fanny and Grattan Guinness their wish to go to China, and he told them to "stay at home and train me the men" (that included for Hudson Taylor the women). They started the East London Training Institute for Evangelists at Home and Abroad", the mother of all Bible Schools. For their history and missionary importance see: Klaus Fiedler, "Aspects of the Early History of the Bible School Movement", in: *Festschrift Donald Moreland. The*

tasks and opportunities to women (single or married) on all levels, and he made theirs a whole province, the Kwang Sin Basin (with an approximate length of 300 km and 15 million inhabitants).[137] Taylor took seriously the understanding that missions must determine the theology of the church, though he would not have used the formula.[138] Just as much as he, who came from the Christian Brethren, offered women all the possibilities, so he also saw ordination as having only personal (not ecclesiastical) value,[139] and the unity of all believers was for him an unquestioned reality practiced daily.[140]

With the China Inland Mission the first Faith Mission was born—in our current theology the first Evangelical Mission—and with it a completely new type of Protestant missions.[141] Frequently these different origins are ignored, and church leaders and even missiologists write that the Evangelicals (maybe in 1910 or maybe in 1961?) separated from the "ecumenical" missions and developed "parallel structures." They could not separate because they had never been one.[142]

Secret of Faith. In Your Heart - In Your Mouth. Marthinus W. Pretorius (ed), Leuven: Evangelical Theological Faculty, 1992, pp. 62-77.

[137] A.J. Broomhall, *Assault on the Nine*, Sevenoaks/London, 1988, pp. 232-251 ('Women Inland'), p. 387, Appendix 1; Howard Taylor, *By Faith. Henry W. Frost and the China Inland Mission*, Singapore, ²1988 (1938), pp. 163-165. – Two German women's missions had their own territories assigned: Eva von Thiele-Winkler's Friedenshort Mission (Kweichow Province) and the Deutsche Frauenmissionsgebetsbund (Shungking in Szechwan Province). See Andreas Franz, *Mission ohne Grenzen. Hudson Taylor und die deutschsprachigen Glaubensmissionen*, Giessen/Basel: Brunnen, 1993.

[138] In later literature we read that Hudson Taylor gave the women of the North American Branch (mainly Canadians) the Kwang Sin Basin because he did not have enough men. But I am sure, had he wanted, he would have found at least one man for the Kwang Sin Basin.

[139] As a young man he once received a Methodist "Preacher's Certificate". Since many could not understand that he was never ordained, he allowed people later even to call him "Reverend". Ordination simply did not matter for him.

[140] Condition for such unity was a simple statement of faith, similar to the "Basis" of the Evangelical Alliance of 1856. Interdenominational cooperation had been quite common in the Classical Missions, but the Faith Missions extended the concept to cooperation between those who held contradictory views on baptism (Infant/believers').

[141] Klaus Fiedler, *The Story of Faith Missions from Hudson Taylor to Present Day Africa*, Oxford et al: Regnum, 1994, "A new missionary movement: the early history of faith missions" (pp. 32-69).

[142] For my assessment of this see: Klaus Fiedler, "The World Missionary Conference 'Edinburgh 1910' as seen from Malawi, *Religion and Culture*, (1), 2013, pp. 23-33.

Such misunderstandings could develop because Evangelicals, though they had always been a movement of their own, had and have an *undelimited identity*.[143] The Evangelicals (as much as their missions) had their own roots (Holiness Revival and parts of the Restorationist Revival), had their own ecclesiastical background (the Fellowship Movements, Free Churches with believers' baptism, evangelical congregations within the mainline churches),[144] their own problems and their own extremists.

Therefore there is no competition with the Classical Missions, and for the same reason there can be no "parallel structures."[145] Therefore we Evangelicals should not steal their fathers,[146] but we should remember our own fathers (plus a few mothers),[147] whom we love to forget.[148] Evangelical separateness ("Eigenständigkeit") implies that we are responsible for our own topics (with conversion

---

[143] Dr McIntire, ICCC President (ICCC claims to be a rival of the WCC) told me, that lack of separation [from evil and from all who do not separate from it] was the crucial point of divergence with Professor Peter Beyerhaus ("otherwise such a good man").

[144] The Faith Missions, though not decided on the issue of baptism, developed in their majority churches which were more of the "gathered church" type. These churches did not become Baptist, but often had many similarities with them, they were "Baptist type" churches, like Africa Inland Church or Zambezi Evangelical Church.

[145] The "Ecumenicals" also have their own structures, and nobody should deny such to them. That the "Ecumenicals" had such structures earlier is a historical priority, not a theological prerogative.

[146] I was never happy that at the "Evangelical Graduate School of Missions" in Korntal, where I started my career as a teacher of missiology, almost all the rooms were named after Classical German missiologists. I have no doubt that Gustav Warneck was a great missiologist, but he didn't like the Evangelicals (this we can easily forgive him because they disturbed what he considered as good order), and, on a more serious note, he wrote a (Classical) Protestant missiology, not an Evangelical one.

[147] During the 25 years of its existence, the Association of German Speaking Evangelical Missiologists has improved things, at least in academic circles. I am not sure how far this has trickled down to the Mission and Church History syllabi. When I visited one of the German speaking schools, I found that they simply taught the history of the Classical Missions with an appendix on the history of the China Inland Mission. Sure, the history of the Classical Missions should be taught in Evangelical schools, but the Evangelical Missions must be presented as movements of their own. – At Mzuzu University the Church History syllabus covers Classical and Evangelical churches equally.

[148] This includes the investigation if the founders of the Faith Missions—these days—would have passed the candidate course. Probably not (for being too extreme).

always in their centre) and for our own agenda.[149] This also implies that we need our own institutions (and that we have to pay for them),[150] and that we need, of course, our own missiology. In German speaking Europe the Association of German Speaking Evangelical Missiologists has been working on that since 25 years and their work and the work of others has achieved something, but there is still so much to do.[151]

11 And then Came the Pentecostals

One of the deep desires of the Holiness Revival was to receive the full blessing of Pentecost, and when that blessing finally came (Los Angeles, Azusa Street, 1906) most of the revivalists were not that happy. It seems to be observable that revivalists feel that their revival must be the best (and therefore the last). Latourette sees things differently, and God seems to be on Latourette's side.

The theology of the Pentecostals is no issue here, but we note that the Pentecostals have become, within a century, the largest Protestant denominational family. Their rapid spread was part of the shift of Christian gravity to the global South, especially through winning many (nominal) Catholics in Latin America.[152]

The Pentecostal missions in Germany remained small, because Pentecostalism in Germany remained small.[153] Though the German Pentecostals remained isolated

---

[149] Not that we should shun dialogue with Ecumenical missiology, but such dialogue must not dominate our (Evangelical) agenda.

[150] To have and own such institutions does not exclude cooperation wherever this is appropriate. Why should an Ecumenical theologian not study at an Evangelical institution? And we do not need to write *all* the books ourselves!

[151] Klaus Fiedler, ""It is Time to Write the History of German Speaking Evangelical Missions", in: Stephan Holthaus and Klaus W. Müller (eds.): *Die Mission der Theologie.* (Festschrift Hans Kasdorf). Bonn: VKW, 1998, pp. 136-151.—It is time indeed to do that, maybe high time!

[152] This reopened the issue—in Edinburgh 1910 decided against the Evangelicals—if Roman Catholic areas can be mission fields. And when in Latin America the Roman Catholic Church (or at least part of it) developed the "Option *for* the Poor", a larger number of the poor chose the Pentecostal message as the "Option *of* the Poor." – On this topic I had the privilege to supervise: Andy Kennedy, A Historical and Missiological Investigation of the Growth of the Assembléia de Deus in Pará, Brazil, from 1980 to 2010, PhD, Evangelical Theological Faculty Leuven, 2013

[153] Joost Reinke: *Deutsche Pfingstmissionen. Geschichte – Theologie – Praxis.* edition afem – mission scripts, vol. 11. Bonn: VKW, 1997. – The isolation has since been overcome.

from "regular" Evangelicalism, they developed a thoroughly Evangelical missiology.[154]

12 A New Evangelical Beginning

Worldwide spiritual movements these days normally start in America and then have their impact outside, with American help or without. While the churches in Europe had to use all their energies to get through the Second World War,[155] important things happened in America. The mainline churches began their theological (and soon also numerical) decline, and the Evangelicals experienced a new period of growth after distancing themselves from the Fundamentalists and creating their own theology[156] and promoting their own institutions.[157] This new and revived Evangelicalism revived the Evangelical Missions Associations (EFMA, IFMA) and the Evangelicals became the leading power in American world missions.

13 And then the Charismatics

Latourette begins the 4th Recession in 1914, and both the First and the Second War did not produce a revival as other wars had done. So he did his thinking and writing when the expansion of the Christian faith had turned into a decline. Western Europe, once the very heart of Christianity, declined religiously. In Eastern Europe Communism had triumphed over National Socialism. America remained Christian and Capitalist,[158] but Europe, in the midst of Capitalist reconstruction, gave, on the one hand, much room to materialism, but at the same time, through a love affair of many young people with Socialism (more with the ideal than the real), deeply questioned every authority, be it political or religious. This movement reached its climax in the students' revolution of 1968.

---

[154] Ulf Strohbehn has been a missionary of the Velbert Mission in Malawi. I supervised his MA thesis, published as Ulf Strohbehn, *Pentecostalism in Malawi: The History of the Apostolic Faith Mission,* Zomba: Kachere, 2005. In December 2010 he successfully defended his PhD: "The Zionist Churches in Malawi. History – Theology – Anthropology", a thorough study to be published by Mzuni Press in 2015.

[155] Due to the war the World Council of Churches (WCC) could be founded only in 1948 in Amsterdam.

[156] Carl F. Henry, *God, Revelation and Authority,* 6 vls, Waco: Word Books, 1983; *Basic Christian Doctrines,* Grand Rapids: Baker, 1979.

[157] Fuller, BIOLA, Trinity, Wheaton etc.

[158] In ever different admixtures.

Just as the Great Awakening began before the Enlightenment had reached its climax (the third recession), so God's answer started eight years before, again in America (as it had always happened since the Great Awakening), and even in California as with the Pentecostal Revival in 1906.

As the beginning of the Charismatic Revival very often the experiences of David Bennet in Van Nuys (California) are taken (1960),[159] and while the Charismatic Revival and the Pentecostal Revival had the same geographical origin and much of a common theology, the two revivals differed in very important aspects: while the Pentecostal Revival originated with the minority population [black in those days in California], had little formal education, was quite at home among the poor and the marginalized, and came from the fringe of the Protestant spectrum (smaller groups of the Holiness Movement), the Charismatic Revival was born among the majority population [white in California in those days], erupted in a mainline church [Anglican],[160] quickly reached the universities and found much allegiance among the middle and upper classes.[161]

Both the Pentecostals and the (traditional) Evangelicals had problems to accept that a new revival brought new (and often challenging) theologies and practices. Just as the Pentecostal Revival had promised the deeper/higher life in the Spirit (and was quickly expelled from most denominations) so the Charismatic Revival promised power through the experience of the Holy Spirit. Different from the 1910s, when the Pentecostal Movement was widely expelled from the churches, the Charismatic Revival often remained within the churches, from mainline Catholic (and even Orthodox) via both Lutherans and Reformed to Baptists of various descriptions.

Sometimes the Charismatic Movement led to Spiritual Renewal movements in many churches,[162] sometimes splits occurred,[163] sometimes a denomination

---

[159] With movements it is often difficult to date the beginning precisely. But often a scholarly consensus emerges, which agrees on a specific event. An example is the dating of the beginning of the Reformation with the nailing of Luther's 95 theses at the door of the Castle Church in Wittenberg, which also served as the notice board for the University.

[160] Soon the movement reached other mainline churches. Different from the Great Awakening, Catholics and Orthodox were reached directly. It is of interest for me that the influence on the Southern Baptists (if the statistics are right with 16 million members the second largest denomination in the USA after the Roman Catholic Church) was limited.

[161] Klaus Fiedler, "The Charismatic and Pentecostal Movements in Malawi in Cultural Perspective", *Religion in Malawi*, no. 9, 1999, pp. 28-38, shows this as it applied to Malawi.

[162] Here in Malawi Blantyre Synod, Anglicans and Roman Catholics were involved.

[163] The birth of Rivers of Life Evangelical Church out of the Evangelical Church in Malawi is a case in point.

developed a "Charismatic branch",[164] and in many cases certain elements were accepted, especially in the area of church music.[165] The new style of worship (no longer a sermon with "sandwich liturgy" but with [long] praise and worship followed by teaching), the Charismatic Revival offered to the Evangelical churches an attractive alternative.[166] At a time when many of the revival people had become glued to their traditions (those that had been highly innovative a few generations ago!), the Charismatic Revival got things moving again and reconciled the educated Christians (and their numbers had been growing tremendously) with the modern world.[167]

Every time a new revival comes, this constitutes a crisis for the proponents (and sometimes survivors) from the last revival. I do not think that it is God's will and guidance that each new revival should replace the previous one (or all the previous ones),[168] but I do think that every revival has to come to terms with the next. If a new revival is completely rejected by the previous one, that seems to be no good for that revival,[169] because it is based on a fixation of (biblically unsupported) traditions. A transition of whole denominations to a new revival is also rare,[170] but Charismatic branches in a "non-charismatic" denomination are quite frequent,[171]

---

[164] This is the case with the Fellowship of Youth of the Zambezi Evangelical Church.

[165] The "Praise Team" is now a feature equally in urban Baptist, Zambezi Evangelical, Pentecostal and Charismatic churches.

[166] Not mentioning different content, Charismatic music is better, more powerful and more attractive.

[167] This was after the attempt by Rudolf Bultmann and his disciples had obviously failed to reach what they called the "modern man." (I wrote my final dissertation at the Baptist Seminary 1965 on Rudolf Bultmann's theology and his missionary intentions.)

[168] After all, what found expression in such revivals was biblical truth!

[169] The Baptists, children of the Puritan Revival had lost much of their revival spirit (many congregations had turned Unitarian), when the Methodist variety of the Great Awakening revived them. Those Baptists who withstood Methodist influences turned Hyper-Calvinist and declined ever after (but they had the truth). See John Briggs, "Early English Baptists" in Tim Dowley (ed), *The History of Christianity*, Oxford/Batavia/Sydney, 1977, pp. 406-409.

[170] Such a case may be the acceptance of Pentecostal theology by the Baptist Örebro Mission in Sweden or the transformation of African Assemblies of God into Cross Life.

[171] In the Roman Catholic Church in Malawi "Our Lady of Africa Prayer Group" in and around Lilongwe (Joe Makaiko Banda, *The Catholic Charismatic Renewal: An Empowerment of the Laity in the Catholic Church in Malawi*", Kachere Documents no. 1, Zomba: Kachere, 2006) is an example. In Zambezi Evangelical Church the "Youth Wing" is also the home of elder Charismatics (Mateyu Saul, *An Analysis of the Rising Conflicts between Youths and Elders in Evangelical Churches: A Case of Zomba Zambezi Evangelical Church*, Zomba: Kachere, 2007).

and it is unavoidable (and I do not regret it at all), that from such Charismatic groups (ministries, fellowships etc) again and again new denominations are born.[172]

In Africa (at least south of the Sahara) the Charismatic Revival has reformatted the Christian landscape. Its strong influence among the educated can not be overlooked, and missiologists who once postulated that the African Independent Churches are the authentic (and future true) expression of the Christian faith in Africa, have to admit their error.[173] Everywhere there emerge new Charismatic churches,[174] and the largest church building in Africa is, of course, home to a Charismatic congregation.[175] That the Charismatic churches in Africa are far more African than the African Independent Churches is due to the fact that in their theology and in their ministry address successfully the three core concerns of African Traditional Religion: the search for health, power and wealth.[176]

---

[172] Living Waters, the largest Charismatic denomination in Malawi, (maybe 100,000 members), was born out of a music group "Living Waters". – For the history of the first Charismatic denomination in Malawi see: Khetwayo Banda, Word Alive Ministries International (WAMI) and its Wholistic Mission, MA, Mzuzu University, 2012.

[173] The argument was that they took African culture so seriously. Hilary Mijoga, my collea-gue at Chancellor College, took this belief ("AICs are vanguards of African culture"), recorded 199 AIC sermons and found nothing of that. As Kachere editor I read all the sermons and concluded that when I preached in the English Service of my Zomba Baptist Church, my sermons would be much more "African" than those of the alleged "vanguards of African culture". (See Hilary Mijoga, *Separate but Same Gospel: Preaching in African Instituted Churches in Southern Malawi*, Blantyre: CLAIM-Kachere, 2000). Among the many denomina-tions from which Hilary Mijoga included sermons there were no Zionists who have devel-oped more "African" forms of the Christian faith. Ulf Strohbehn shows the Zionists' attrac-tion for the Ngoni of the Central Region and the South (not for those of Mzimba) but also that they can hardly get a foothold in town and lose the youth in many cases (Ulf Strohbehn, The Zionist Churches in Malawi, PhD, University of Malawi 2010; to be published as *The Zionist Churches in Malawi: History – Theology – Anthropology*, Mzuzu: Mzuni Press, 2015).

[174] According to a rough estimate, 5% of all Christians in Malawi are Charismatics.

[175] In Lagos, 40,000 Sunday attendance. For West Africa see Bosco Bangura, The Charismatic Movement in Sierra Leone: Missio-historical analysis in view of African Culture, Prosperity Gospel and Power Theology, PhD, Evangelical Theological Faculty Leuven, 2013.

[176] Matthews Ojo, *The End-Time Army. Charismatic Movements in Modern Nigeria*, Trenton: Africa World Press, 2006. – This does not mean that non-Charismatics should copy everything Charismatic, since every revival has its own extremists (and must deal with them!). Prayer for healing is biblical, and God has given impressive healings, but to make healing depending on full tithing is not biblical. In extreme cases the teaching is that healing received will be lost if the healed patient stops paying the tithe. - A new variety of fake healings has come up in *some* branches of the Charismatic Movement: A prophet prays for someone HIV+, pronounces her or him instantly healed, decrees that no ARVs be taken

In terms of worldwide missions, the vision of the Charismatics is comprehensive, though the reality is less grand than the vision. Their ideas are often innovative (typical for revivals), but there is also much wastage, while new ways are being explored (equally typical for revivals).[177] In Germany the Charismatic Missions have formed their own "mother body", a development which we Evangelicals (of the more traditional variety) welcome in the spirit of Christian unity, and more cooperation should develop.[178]

14 Edinburgh 1910/2010

In 2010 much attention was paid to Edinburgh 1910, and indeed, the largest mission conference that has ever taken place deserved that attention. The concern of the conference was the evangelization of the Non-Christian world. That was seen as an imminent possibility at that time, and the big breakthrough was expected in Asia. This breakthrough took long to come, and when it came, after two world wars and one Cultural Revolution, it took forms very different from those envisaged in Edinburgh 60 years before.[179] While Edinburgh 1910 was watching for the break

---

forthwith and the healed patient dies a few months later of AIDS. One of my students found several such deaths, a number of *claims* to healing, but no willingness at all to have the healing tested (Manly Mkonda Phiri, Analyzing Critical HIV and AIDS Results in Malawi: A Case Study of an Interface between Faith/Traditional Healing Claims and Scientific Treatment, BA, Mzuzu University, 2014). Another student found the secular variety of fake healing in the Voluntary Male Medical Circumcision Campaign (Joseph Alufandika, The Voluntary Medical Male Circumcision (VMMC) Campaign: Dissemination and Impact. A Case Study of T/A Mbenje in Nsanje-Southern Malawi, BA, Mzuzu University, 2013).

[177] A clear success of Charismatic Missions is the evangelization of African migrants in Europe and America. One of these migrants, Kibutu Ngimbi, is the pastor of the largest Evangelical congregation in Brussels. I supervised his PhD on the Charismatic Movement in Kinshasa and on its effects overseas (Kibutu Ngimbi, Les Nouvelles Églises Indépendantes Africaines [NAIC]. Un phénomène ecclésial observé au Congo/Kinshasa et auprès de ses extensions en Europe occidentale, ETF: Leuven, 2000).

[178] Their leader is Andreas Franz, my first doctoral student at the Evangelical Theological Faculty in Leuven. His thesis was published as: Andreas Franz, *Mission ohne Grenzen. Hudson Taylor and die deutschsprachigen Glaubensmissionen* Giessen/Basel: Brunnen, 1993.

[179] Edinburgh 1910 was a conference of the mainline churches and their missions from the Great Awakening, and the breakthrough was expected as a consequence of the Christian superiority (and the missions had achieved a lot with their schools and hospitals). When the breakthrough finally came, there were no missionaries left in China, there was no idea of intellectual superiority, and the revival took predominantly Evangelical (and sometimes Charismatic) forms. (I am aware that this is some simplification!)

through in Asia, it ignored that the very thing they were hoping for was happening full force in Africa.[180]

Instead of celebrating what God was doing in Africa, the conference report (vol. 1) lamented that not only was 1/3 of Africa completely unreached, but that not a single mission had even plans to advance into that area. Here the conference was not only wrong in its vision, but equally so on facts. The Church Missionary Society (one of the Classical Missions) had started to advance into the Sudan Belt, and that was overlooked. More serious a mistake was to take no note of the efforts of the Faith Missions (since 1873) to reach that remaining third of Africa that had not been reached by the Classical Missions. These missions did not only have plans to reach the remaining third of Africa, they were busy doing it.

The reports of the conference are normally quite reliable, but this error shows the problems of the conference. Since I have written about Edinburgh 1910 already,[181] here I simply list the major points.

1. Edinburgh 1910 was organized by the Classical Missions (born in the Great Awakening).

2. The Evangelicals were cordially invited under the condition that they accept the classical (sacramental) concept of the church.

3. This meant that missionary work in Catholic areas (especially Latin America) had to be excluded form the discussions of the conference, since all people there were Christians (at least in the sacramental sense).

4. The Evangelical Missions participated (with less than 5% of the delegates, and none among the leaders and the special [appointed] delegates) and made no fuss, but it was not their conference.

5. The conference made a decisive turn, moving the aim of missions from reaching the Non-Christians (Commission 1) to reaching the unity of all Christians (Commission 8).[182]

---

[180] That was true for those two thirds of Africa which had been reached by the Classical Missions. Almost everywhere the number of baptized Christians was small, but everywhere the Christian churches were the dominant religious force. It was also overlooked that the missions had brought to a stop (around 1910) the Muslim advance in Africa.

[181] Klaus Fiedler, "Edinburgh 2010 and the Evangelicals," *Evangelical Theological Review*, 34/4 (Oct 2010). pp. 53-71).

[182] This unity was necessary, of course, to reach the non-Christians more effectively. But since to achieve that unity might take an eternity, until then the unreached would not profit from that unity.

6. Therefore it was simple logic that out of Edinburgh 1910 not only came the International Missionary Council, but also (increasingly prominent) the World Council of Churches.

7. That New Delhi 1961 decided to dissolve the International Missionary Council and to integrate its interests into the World Council of Churches was the logical (and disastrous) consequence of the turn the Edinburgh conference had decided to make.

8. The Evangelicals were not really part of the Edinburgh conference, and the turn that was made there explains (and justifies) why the Evangelical gradually gave up any participation in the International Missionary Council.[183]

14.1 Evangelicals and the Ecumenical Missions

Edinburgh 2010 offered a chance to approach each other again. Both groups of missions are children of revivals, but of different ones. For this reason they were never one, and the claim of one group (even an important one), to represent the whole, is never justified, neither is it here. There were two streams of missions, right from the beginning.

Edinburgh made the decisive difference clear (the concept of the church) and, probably helped by the Anglican wish to keep its various branches together, showed the Evangelicals where they belonged.[184] The conference (and the movement that came out of it) gave unity priority over missions, and the sacrament priority over faith, thus pushing the revival heritage into the background or even giving it up.[185]

---

[183] The China Inland Mission was offered a seat on the Continuation Committee, but they refused. In Jerusalem I could not find any representative of an Evangelical mission, in Tambaram (1938) I found three, if I interpret the list of participants correctly (three Swedish missionaries in Central Asia).

[184] To exclude the discussion of missionary work among Catholics was the small price the conference was willing to pay to secure the full participation of the Anglican Church with its three traditions (Anglo-Catholic, Broad Church and Evangelical) and all the bishops and archbishops.

[185] The influence of the Student Volunteer Movement was considerable in Edinburgh (John Mott belonged to it) with its endeavour to achieve the "evangelization of the world in this generation." The Student Christian Movement, its successor organization, showed two generations later only historical knowledge of this, when in 1985 in Edinburgh a memorial conference was held. See Klaus Müller, "Auf der Suche nach einem größeren Christus (In Search of a Larger Christ"). Studenten-Missions-Konferenz Edinburgh/Schottland, 24.-26.6.1985. 75 Jahre nach der ersten Weltmissionskonferenz in Edinburgh 1910,"

The new directions taken at Edinburgh 1910 found their full fulfillment after World War II, when the concept of the church that who is baptized is a Christian, supported by more "liberal" forms of theology and aided by growing materialism led to a dramatic realignment of Western European missiology.[186]

This decline happened parallel to a new (world) missionary departure among Evangelicals. That they created their own structures for that was to be expected, was a necessity and a blessing. This is no reason to be haughty, but an encouragement to build God's kingdom in all humility. And in this humility we also know that we are neither the only ones nor the most beautiful ones doing that, and therefore we can, with our own undelimited identity, exchange our views and cooperate with all who work to build the same Kingdom of God, though they may be doing that in very different corners.

Where we do our work should be informed by the concept that missions are the theology of the church. Because, if there is rejoicing in heaven over one sinner who repents, we should work hard to increase that heavenly joy.

While we work for that joy to increase, the theological principle of "missions as the theology of the church" may help us to solve some tricky theological problems. I will deal with only a few, and since I am a historian, I will do it along the lines of church history.[187] I have chosen five pertinent topics: (1) Predestination (2) The role of women in God's kingdom (3) Christian unity (4) wholistic mission and (5) migration.

Evangelikale Missiologie, 1986,7-13. At the end Klaus Müller gives this summary: "What the "Larger Christ" was, was difficult to discern. They were searching for Him, outside the Word of God, and got lost in politics, sociology, ecumenism and economics. The net they cast was so wide, that it could not catch the "old Christ" (whom we might find in John 3:16 and 14:6). Before the service started, I asked a student from Sri Lanka about his opinion of the conference. Without hesitating Darshan Ambalavanar answered: "Maybe it is true that the 1910 conference saw mission too much in a spiritual way, but this time definitely mission was too much defined by material and economic issues."

[186] In his contribution to Edinburgh 2010 Andrew Walls emphasizes that European theology currently has no chance to take a leading role in world missions. "The Western theological academy is at present not well placed for leadership in the new situation." (Andrew Walls, "Commission One and the Church's Transforming Century" in: David A. Kerr and Kenneth R. Ross (eds), *Edinburgh 2010. Mission Then and Now*, Oxford: Regnum, 2009, pp. 27-40 [38]).

[187] But since church history only ends today, I hope that historical considerations can be of some use even today.

15 Missions as the Theology of the Church and Predestination

The issue of predestination may not interest us today that much, and what was a few generations ago a device to split denominations, may not even feature in church union talks today. I am convinced that the issue of predestination and free will can not (and should not) be resolved by systematic theological argumentation, because divine reality is much advanced (by one or more dimensions) over what we call "reality". Therefore I propose a missiological solution as possible (and adequate). Here again history (and Latourette) may guide us.

During the Reformation Calvin solved the problem in his own systematic way, maybe because as a man trained in Law he could not agree to leave loose ends dangling.[188] Calvin did not have much to do with missions, though he had nothing against them.[189] When the vivid revivals of the Reformations began to harden into orthodox theologies, the Lutherans were so taken up by fighting the idea that the Pope might be the "successor to the apostles" that they declared foreign missions to be sin[190] and that many Calvinists developed "Hyper-Calvinism" with the right doctrine at the centre, and be it at the cost of the existence of the church.[191]

Indeed, if the Calvinistic doctrine of "double predestination" is taken seriously,[192] there is no need for missions, since whom God elected He will also

---

[188] That is how my (Anglican) lecturer in Dogmatics at Makerere University, expressed it.

[189] This was similar with Martin Luther, who did not teach double predestination, but who, as a disciple of Augustine, did not teach free will.

[190] See the Wittenberg theological advice of 1652 (*Consilia theologica Witebergensia, Das ist Wittenbergische Geistliche Rathschläge deß theuren Mannes Gottes D. Martini Lutheri, seiner Collegen and treuen Nachfolger*, Frankfurt 1664, quoted in Werner Raupp, *Mission in Quellentexten. Von der Reformation bis zur Weltmissionskonferenz 1910*, Erlangen/Bad Liebenzell: Verlag der Evang.-Luth. Mission/Verlag der Liebenzeller Mission, 1990, p. 70f.)

[191] In Zambia this variation of Baptists is represented by the Reformed Baptists who are convinced that the Baptist Confession of 1689 is the only correct expression of Baptist (and therefore biblical) faith. (As if Baptists had ever believed in binding confessions of faith!) Congregations who called pastors from that background, declined in numbers and outreach. For dramatic descriptions see Reinhard Frey, *The History of the Zambia Baptist Association*, Zomba: Kachere, 2007, pp. 139, 148, 153f. A printed version of this confession (the third in Baptist history) is: "The Baptist Confession of Faith 1689: Update with notes by Dr Peter Masters and Proof Texts", Johannesburg: Precision Print, undated. In Germany there may be two such churches, in Malawi a few, in Zambia many. Historically they may be Baptists, but tragically they have exchanged the basic Baptist endeavour to bring people to salvation with the basic endeavour to bring them to the truth.

[192] This includes "irresistible grace" and "perseverance of the saints" (once saved, forever saved!)#

make to persevere till eternity, with or without the church. Revivals, aiming to make the sinner repent, can't go that way. John Wesley, deeply concerned with human salvation,[193] chose the Arminian way,[194] and he found much sympathy among revival leaders. John Wesley won his friend George Whitefield to the new level of the Christian faith, and Whitefield became one of the greatest revival preachers,[195] but remained a Calvinist.[196] Charles Haddon Spurgeon, who built up the largest congregation of his time in London, always remained a Calvinist, but was a great evangelist and told his (Baptist and other) friends that for the love of God they had to give up their Hyper-Calvinism.[197]

Like many of the revivalists, Jonathan Edwards could not give up his Calvinism, but he redefined the doctrine of election in a way to *include* human responsibility into it.[198]

Robert Moffat, the pioneer missionary among the Tswana in Kuruman, went into another direction. He simply ignored predestination in his theology and centred it on the glory of God and how to promote it.[199]

Such a blessed ignoring of the issue of predestination was also practiced by Spencer Walton, one of the founders of the South Africa General Mission. He declared that his young missionaries were no trained theologians, and for them [and him] it did not matter if someone was saved Calvinistically or Arminianistically.

To me such contradictions seem to be a good (mission) theology as they can leave aside the theological controversies. To me geography gives a helpful example. Since the earth is a globe, all maps, of necessity, are false because they lack one (essential) dimension. Why should I take the trouble to decide if the Mercator projection is correct or the more recent Peters projection? If I want to sail

---

[193] To achieve that, he travelled the length of three times around the world, loved to preach three times a day in three different places, and happily ignored the (almost sacred) Anglican parochial system. ("My parish is the world").

[194] The theological journal, which he edited for several years, was titled "The Arminian".

[195] From him Wesley learned open air preaching.

[196] This led top a serious quarrel between them, but they managed to get beyond that, since for both conversion was more important than correct dogmatics.

[197] I like Spurgeon very much [I translated and edited his autobiography into German] because he taught Calvinism and lived Armenianism. (I know he would have refused such an interpretation...). – C.H. Spurgeon, *Alles zur Ehre Gottes. Autobiographie*, Wuppertal/Kassel: Oncken, 1984.

[198] The Evangelical Theological Faculty in Leuven, where I have been (Guest) Professor since 1990, is establishing a Jonathan Edwards Research Centre.

[199] B. Ritchie, The Theology of Robert Moffat of Kuruman, PhD, University of Malawi, 2006.

the oceans (which I never even dreamt of) I would use Mercator's projections,[200] if I want to understand the sizes of continents and countries, I choose Peters.[201] And Dwight Lyman Moody, the great Evangelist, said: "When we approach the door of salvation, we read on it: 'Decide,' when we have passed the door and turn around, we read on it 'elected from the beginning of the world.'"

I appreciate such contradictory systematic theologies, as they get close to the core of the Christian message, to missions, and as contradictory as they are, they seem to come closer to the truth. It is a strength in Evangelical theology not to follow appropriate logic.

17 The Position of Women in the Kingdom of God

One of the distinct characteristics of Evangelicals is their love for the Bible, and some of them, in reading the book, came to conclusions that woman must keep her mouth shut in church (but may sing),[202] or that she may not teach (or may not teach *men*)[203] or that she may not exercise authority over men.[204]

Just as much as the Evangelicals love the Bible, they are children of revival(s), and in that context it obviously pleased the Holy Spirit to give women many gifts and tasks, responsibilities and privileges. Church history shows this: When revival comes, the differences between men and women do not disappear, but they are

---

[200] The school atlas of my sisters, Ursula and Melitta, which made the world fascinating for me in the first decade of my life, was Dierke's Weltatlas, of course with Mercator projection.

[201] And I take the liberty to ignore the Socialist/Communist ideology of his thematic maps.

[202] That was the rule in Hamburg Brethren Assembly to which I belonged while studying at the Baptist Seminary. Never would a woman pray (aloud) during the weekly prayer meeting, but they did sing in the choir. When *Reformed* Baptist theology spread among the revived students in Lusaka Baptist Church, some female students felt obliged to leave the choir, as singing with it to a mixed audience meant "teaching men" (Reinhard Frey, *History of the Zambia Baptist Association 1905-2005*, Zomba: Kachere, 2009).

[203] With this version the problem arises to define when a *male child* becomes a *man*. For women in youth ministry the problem is to decide when a boy (whom she can teach as a child) turns into a man (whom she must not teach), maybe at 12 (age of religious majority in Germany) or at 14 (average age of first discharge of semen) or at 18 (legal majority in many countries) or at 21 (that is when I reached legal majority in 1963)?

[204] In the English Charismatic House Church Movement, where everyone has to be under someone's authority ("covering"), the problem is solved by putting every woman under the "cover" of a man, while no woman can provide any "cover" for a man.

reduced.²⁰⁵ Then the question is no longer how a complicated passage in Scripture may be interpreted, but which role women can play in the evangelization of the world (at home and abroad). The method "Missions as the Theology of the Church" can be applied here without problems. A few examples may show this:

John Wesley was an Anglican priest, before and after his "conversion," when "his heart was strangely warmed" and he became the great evangelist of God's grace. When in his Methodist societies women started no longer to keep properly quiet, he told them to be quiet. That they didn't do (for revival people that is difficult), and soon Wesley realized that God blessed their participation. He stopped to advise them to keep quiet, and as time went on, he encouraged them more and more in their ministry, and one of them he even gave the Preacher's Certificate, at that time the highest "rank" a Methodist could attain. When Wesley, then advanced in age, was asked why he, as an Anglican priest, could allow women to preach, he answered: "If God owns them in the conversion of sinners, who am I to hinder Him."²⁰⁶

Fredrik Franson, the international evangelist and promoter of missions (1852-1908),²⁰⁷ commissioned by Moody's Chicago Avenue Church in Chicago, was confronted with the "problem" of women's preaching when he evangelized in Sweden. There was a young woman, Nellie Hall, evangelizing just like he did. He was asked for his opinion on that thing. He asked for a bit of time to think and read his Bible. When the time of thinking was over, he was asked again, and he replied: "Those working in the harvest are but few, and if women want to help to bring in some sheaves, we surely should allow them." And when he was asked how that would reconcile with 1 Corinthians 14 and 1 Timothy 2, he answered: "These are two passages difficult to understand, and maybe after some time the Holy Spirit may shed some light on them, and until that happens, let the women evangelize."²⁰⁸

---

²⁰⁵ For a study along these lines see: Frank Chirwa, A Critical Examination of the Changing Role of Women in the Seventh-day Adventist Church in Malawi: A Historical, Theological and Socio-Cultural Analysis, PhD, Mzuzu University, 2014.

²⁰⁶ Paul Wesley Chilcote, *John Wesley and the Women Preachers of Early Methodism*, PhD, Duke University, 1984 (UMI).

²⁰⁷ He encouraged hundreds of young people to become missionaries, many of them with the CIM in China.

²⁰⁸ Franson was probably the first to publish a book in Germany that promoted the preaching of women. Fredrik Franson, *Weissagende Töchter*, Emden 1890; also *Gemeinschaftsblatt*, Emden, no. 16 and 17, 1890. Swedish editions (*Profeterande Döttrar*) appeared in 1896 (St Paul) and in 1897 (Stockholm).

Catherine Booth, with her husband William founder of the Salvation Army, got the news that Phoebe Palmer, one of the "founders" of the Holiness Movement,[209] together with husband Walther,[210] had come from America to Britain to teach about holiness and that the Anglican priest in one of the towns had objected and preached against that on the next Sunday, (and was kind enough to have his sermon printed), she was furious and decided to travel to that very town and give a lecture that women have the right to preach the Gospel (if they want to do it – she was not interested). Then she realized that she was far too pregnant (with her fourth child) for that journey, so she decided to write a book instead. When her husband came back two weeks later from an evangelistic trip, she showed him the manuscript. He was thrilled and proposed to have it published.[211] At that time Catherine Booth had never preached and had no intention ever to do so.[212] She simply wanted to make it clear what the Gospel says and what the truth is. Later on the Booths founded the Salvation Army in which women and men have always been equal.[213] Her husband William was the first General, the fourth General was their daughter Evelyn (1934-1939).[214]

Bessie Fricker, the founder of the Evangelical Church of Guinea-Bissau, was also a fruit of the revival. She came from Inner London (Arthur's Mission), at Birkenhead Bible School she had to learn proper English first, and she heard the call to missionary work in Guinea Bissau together with some young men. Since she was the only women in that group, she had to go to another land to learn Portuguese than the men, and the men should be the first there and prepare for her as well. The men went first, but they felt that they could not cope with work in that colony. Before Bessie Fricker could join them, they had given up on the call they had earlier received. Norman Grubb wanted to send her the money to return to UK as well,

---

[209] For her theology see: Phoebe Palmer, *The Way of Holiness*, Boston, [50]1867.

[210] Dr Walter Palmer was a practicing medical doctor and at the same time one of the "teachers" of the early Holiness Movement. Like his wife he was a preacher of holiness, but he attracted less attention than his wife, who, in addition, also published a number of books.

[211] Catherine Booth, *Female Ministry; or, Woman's Right to Preach the Gospel*, London, 1859.

[212] Helped by her husband and encouraged by the leaders of her congregation, she took, after some time, the first halting steps. Thereafter she became one of the leading women preachers of her time. Small in statue, she made large crowds listen attentively.

[213] For a time this rule was compromised a little by the decision that a wife could not hold a higher rank than her husband.

[214] Before that she was responsible for cadet training, was commander for the USA, commander for Canada etc. The Wikipedia website "Evangeline Booth" gives a good overview of her life.

but she refused: "You did not send me but God", and Norman Grubb had the spiritual maturity to believe her and he offered her forthwith all possible support to go it alone.[215] When later on Leslie Brierley, WEC missionary in neighbouring Senegal, asked her to marry him, she accepted the offer, provided that he would agree to move to Guinea-Bissau.[216] They worked there according to their gifts, she was more the preacher,[217] and he was more the organizer.

During my research I went there to find out how today the position of women is in a church started by a woman. I asked the elder Amaro. He hesitated a bit with his answer, saying that, according to the Bible, women should be quiet. Then he hesitated again a little and said: "But if the woman hadn't preached, I wouldn't have been saved." He was one of the converts of the Pastora, and he felt it better to have found Christ through a women than not at all.[218]

Critics may intervene here and argue that such "applied theology" lacks the necessary and correct exegesis, but who has the power to decide that theological decisions must be arrived at by "correct" exegesis?[219] When Peter granted the Gentiles *direct* access to the Gospel, had he followed "correct" exegesis he might well have come to the conclusion, assisted by a bit of Rabbinic theology, that the Gospel, after all, is accessible to everyone, they just need to become Jews, and then they can be baptized any time and quickly so. How grateful are we Gentiles that Peter did not go the path of "correct" exegesis!

18 Missions as Theology of the Church and Christian Unity

Edinburgh 1910 assumed, and John Mott formulated it explicitly, that only an (organizationally) united Christianity could ever be capable of evangelizing the non-Christian world. Neither John Mott nor the conference made any effort to support

---

[215] At that time the people at WEC created the slogan: "If a job is too hard for men, God sends a woman." – In many less innovative missions that slogan could never have been coined.

[216] They married in 1945. See also: Klaus Fiedler, "Frauen in Glaubensmissionen", *Weltweit*, 4.2013, p. 26.

[217] Even today she is remembered as the *Pastora* (Int Benvinda Vaz, 5.8.1986).

[218] I am convinced the angels in heaven shared that opinion and rejoiced!

[219] What, after all, is "right exegesis"? As far as the position of women is concerned, among serious readers of the Bible, there are different and contradictory readings, each seriously held as correct. I therefore prefer to solve the problem of women's position in the church from the angle of systematic theology. Does God not want that "all men be saved and come to a knowledge of the truth" (1 Timothy 2:4). If God is so keen on that, does he mind if a (male) man finds that truth with the help of a (female) man? I do not think so!

this assumption from either experience or history. William Carey, the father of modern world missions (and thereby the great-grandfather of Edinburgh 1910) had seen it differently: He felt it to be an unnecessary (and likely fruitless) effort to *promote* missions through church unity. After having proposed a mission society to be formed among the Particular Baptists, thinking that he had the best chances of success in his own denomination, he wrote:

> I do not mean by this, in any wise to confine it to one denomination of Christians. I wish with all my heart that every one who loves our Lord Jesus Christ in sincerity, would in some way or other engage in it. But in the present divided state of Christendom, it would be more likely for good to be done by each denomination engaging separately in the work, than if they were to embark in it conjointly. There is room enough for us all, without interfering with each other; and if no unfriendly interference took place, each denomination would bear good will to the other, and wish, and pray for its success, considering it as upon the whole friendly to the great cause of true religion; but if all were intermingled, it is likely their private discords might throw a damp upon their spirits, and much retard their public usefulness.[220]

He did not promote disunity among Christians, but argued that they should not take the dogmatic (and historical) differences that seriously and that they should not spend their (anyhow limited) resources to remove such minor problems. For him missions had priority, not unity, an idea that in Edinburgh 1910 would have had a small chance as a minority vote.

It is being argued that non-Christians would accept the Christian faith much more easily if all Christians would believe exactly (or almost exactly) the same thing.[221] And how nice would it be if they also had the same name, the same sacraments and the same style of worship. The Lima process shows how difficult it is even to achieve even a limited "convergence",[222] but even if the success rate would be higher,[223] I do not see that as a goal worth struggling for, because humans are quite different, and if their conversion to Jesus Christ is the first and

---

[220] William Carey, *An Enquiry into the Obligations of Christians to Use Means for the Conversion of the Heathens*, Leicester: Ann Ireland, 1792, p. 84.

[221] To support such opinions there can always be found a non-Christian friend who has said such a thing. But that someone shares my opinion is no proof that I am right.

[222] This convergence is offered only to those churches which recognize the "threefold office" (probably Anglican style), as if Baptists, Charismatics, Pentecostals or the Brethren would be able to do that!

[223] Since 1910 there has been a limited number of church unions (mostly of declining churches), but during the same time an incomparably higher number of new denominations was born.

most important goal, then churches are needed as different as people are. It is plurality not unity that promotes missions. And Africa was not evangelized (and successfully so) by the rather monolithic Protestant churches of Europe, but by the very different (and sometimes even contradictory) mission societies, which were not appreciated that much by the churches as long as the societies were successful.

Is it that Evangelicals oppose Christian unity? Often they are more united than some of their Ecumenical friends, since they are looking for spiritual unity which does not require organic (organizational) unity. With this conviction they have preserved the revival heritage, and it is the foundational concern of all revivals that as many people as possible find salvation in Jesus Christ.

Another error is that competition hampers Christian progress. Much of the Communist ideology was based on that assumption, and history's verdict was negative.[224] I am convinced that through Christian pluralism (with all competition and cooperation) more people will be reached with the Gospel than through Christian unity. Spiritual unity with other Christians is a theological aim and a necessary one, even with Christians who follow Christ in very different ways, but organizational unity is a practical aim that should be pursued wherever it is useful,[225] useful to reach more people with the Gospel.[226]

For these historical and theological reasons I see no justification to understand Jesus' prayer for the unity of all his followers (Jh 17:20-21) as a prayer for their organizational ("organic") unity.[227]

---

[224] In spite of the friendship that several "Ecumenical" theologians developed with Socialism (in its various forms).

[225] Here I may add a little (true) anecdote: At the time of the Great Awakening in Wuppertal (50 km from where I grew up) there were born two new congregations, one Baptist and one Free Evangelical, quite similar in many things. They thought about uniting, but did not manage because of different views on baptism. But when it became necessary to acquire a new cemetery (as the Reformed Church did not like to bury non-Reformed on theirs), the two congregations established a joint cemetery. This shows that one has only to be dead enough to be united. – Leaving the realm of jokes, I think of Denmark. The Christians there are extremely united (over 90% are members of the Lutheran Church), with one of the lowest church attendances in the world.

[226] Therefore Mission Councils, Associations and Organizations are useful, as long as there are no claims like "We represent all". Therefore Evangelical Associations are no "parallel structures," but agencies of cooperation in their own right.

[227] But I understand it as a prayer that we should not deny fellowship to anyone who belongs to Christ (and Evangelicals have not always followed Jesus' advice on this point, unfortunately.)

19 What about "Wholistic Mission?"

What I applied to the three areas so far may also be applied to the current topic (or slogan?) of "wholistic mission." I am no great friend of the concept because it often comes along with the assumption that it is something new (and therefore good). For me as a historian wholistic mission is nothing new, definitely not in Africa, where all the early missions applied the triple approach of school, hospital and church.[228] Even here in Malawi, where the government makes quite some effort, one third of the medical care is still in the hands of the various churches.

The early missionaries were deeply wholistic, only that they did not talk much about that (using current terminology), and when they wrote home innocently that medical treatment helped some people to find access to the Christian faith, they are now accused, sometimes at least, that they did all the medical work to make it a bait to capture (otherwise reluctant) Africans.[229]

That the early missionaries were very wholistic should not stop us today from being equally wholistic. The criterion is conversion. Wholistic missions are as necessary today as they were then, and of course forms and structures today may differ. That is all fine. The crucial point is that the central idea must always be the effort to win people for Christ. As long as the core remains intact, this is in order, even when, under specific circumstances, the distance until the core is reached may be considerable; but when "wholistic mission" gives up the hard core of conversion, what remains is a Social Gospel, that soon will be just social, but no longer gospel.[230]

20 Migration and the Unity of the Church

The tremendous migrations that affected Western Europe and other Western countries after World War II also produced a big challenge to the churches' concepts of unity there. The two folk-churches in Germany were built around the

---

[228] Even today much of this is still true, though often the government has taken over many schools and hospitals. Ekwendeni Mission (Church of Central Africa Presbyterian), now over 100 years old, has a hospital, a school of nursing, a major girls' secondary school among others. For the history see: Lisungu Agnes Kachali Mughogho, A Brief History of Ekwendeni Mission Station of the CCAP Synod of Livingstonia: Its Development and Impact, 1889 to 2010, BTh, University of Livingstonia, 2010. (Available as a Mzuni Document).

[229] Such arguments do not only speak against the missionaries, but also deny Africans the ability to decide for any faith.

[230] It is not astonishing that churches that tend to go this way rather lose members than win them.

territorial parochial principle, where the place you live determines the parish you belong to, so an immigrant would join that very parish. That seems to have worked for the Roman Catholic Church, at least to some extent, when immigrants from Italy, Spain and Portugal moved to West Germany. On the Protestant side it usually did not work that way, as immigrants from overseas with a Protestant background often did not find their way to the "appropriate" parish church, but started or joined churches which reflected their cultural background.[231] Sometimes the migrants did not form their own denominations but their own congregations, so the Moravian congregations in the Netherlands increased from one to nine, with the additional congregations composed of Surinamese immigrants.

Often the "Protestant" difficulty was compounded by theological differences. Many of the African, Asian and Latin American Protestants were of the Evangelical variety, and often particularly of the Pentecostal and Charismatic subgroups. So they formed their own congregations, which often satisfied both cultural and spiritual needs.

These churches born in migration have different characteristics, some are mono-cultural, some are multi-cultural, some are international by design, and what they have in common is that there is little room for them in the traditional church system in Europe. This means that they split the church even further. And here my verdict is very clear: If God uses them in the conversion of sinners, that is the highest value. Unity can be sought after that, in so many ways and in so many forms. This means that we don't have to measure these churches with the yardstick of how well integrated they are with the churches in Belgium or in Switzerland, but how many sinners they reach for Christ, be they German, African or Chinese. And I would also be interested in how they keep that attitude into the next generation.

21 Keep the Revival

I am convinced that the Holy Spirit uses again and again revivals to drive forward the history of the church. It is the revivals (and of course their children) that win people to faith in Christ. As a historian I want to understand and describe that, and as a disciple I want to be there when they crown him King of Kings.

---

[231] For a convincing analysis of this process from Switzerland see: Johannes Müller, "Wie gehen Gemeinden in Europa mit kulturellen Unterschieden um?" in *Evangelikale Missiologie* 30[2014]3, pp. 135-153.

Bibliography

Unpublished

Alufandika, Joseph, The Voluntary Medical Male Circumcision (VMMC) Campaign: Dissemination and Impact. A Case Study of T/A Mbenje in Nsanje-Southern Malawi, BA, Mzuzu University, 2013

Banda, Joe Makaiko, The Catholic Charismatic Renewal: An Empowerment of the Laity in the Catholic Church in Malawi, BA Theology, University of Malawi, 2000.

Banda, Macleard "The Remnant and its Mission." An Investigation into the Interaction of the Seventh-day Adventist Church with Society in Malawi, PhD, Mzuzu University, 2014.

Brandl, Bernd, Die Geschichte der Neukirchener Mission als erste deutsche Glaubensmission, PhD, Evangelical Theological Faculty, Leuven, 1997

Chilcote, Paul Wesley, John Wesley and the Women Preachers of Early Methodism, PhD, Duke University, 1984 (UMI).

Chirwa, Frank, A Critical Examination of the Changing Role of Women in the Seventh-day Adventist Church in Malawi: A Historical, Theological and Socio-Cultural Analysis, PhD, Mzuzu University, 2014.

Kachali Mughogho, Lisungu Agnes, A Brief History of Ekwendeni Mission Station of the CCAP Synod of Livingstonia: Its Development and Impact, 1889 to 2010, BTh, University of Livingstonia, 2010.

Kawamba, Bright, The Blantyre Spiritual Awakening 1969 to 1986: an Antecedent of the Charismatic Movement in Malawi, MA, University of Malawi 2013.

Ngimbi, Kibutu, Les Nouvelles Églises Indépendantes Africaines [NAIC]. Un phénomène ecclésial observé au Congo/Kinshasa et auprès de ses extensions en Europe occidentale, Evangelical Theological Faculty, Leuven, 2000).

Phiri, Manly Mkonda, Analyzing Critical HIV and AIDS Results in Malawi: A Case Study of an Interface between Faith/Traditional Healing Claims and Scientific Treatment, BA, Mzuzu University, 2014.

Ritchie, Bruce, The Theology of Robert Moffat of Kuruman, PhD, University of Malawi, 2006.

Sommer, Gottfried, Die 'Belowianer' in Hinterpommern. Ihr Weg vom enthusiastischen Aufbruch zur Bildung einer Freikirche, PhD, Evangelische Theologische Faculteit Leuven, 2010.

Strohbehn, Ulf, The Zionist Churches in Malawi. History – Theology - Anthropology, PhD, University of Malawi, 2010. Publication expected for 2015.

Published

Barclay, Oliver R., Simeon and the Evangelical Tradition, np: Focus, 1988.

Been, Dan, The Changing Role of Women in the Three Main Branches of the *Stone/Campbell Restoration Movement*, Zomba: Kachere, 2011.

Booth, Catherine, *Female Ministry; or, Woman's Right to Preach the Gospel*, London: 1859.

Booth, Joseph, *Africa for the African*, Blantyre: CLAIM-Kachere, ³1997 [¹1897 Lynchburg].

Brandl, Bernd, *Die Neukirchener Mission. Ihre Geschichte als erste deutsche Glaubensmission*, Köln: Rheinland Verlag; Neukirchen-Vluyn, Verlag des Erziehungsvereins, 1998.

Bredekamp, H.C., A.B.L Flegg and Plüdderman (eds), *The Genadendal Diaries*, vol 1, Bellville: University of the Western Cape, 1992.

Briggs, John, "Early English Baptists" in Tim Dowley (ed), *The History of Christianity*, Oxford/Batavia/Sydney, 1977, pp. 406-409.

Broomhall, A.J., *Assault on the Nine*, Sevenoaks/London, 1988, pp. 232-251 ('Women Inland').

Carey, William, *An Enquiry into the Obligations of Christians to Use Means for the Conversion of the Heathens*, Leicester: Ann Ireland, 1792.

Carey: William, *Eine Untersuchung über die Verpflichtung der Christen, Mittel einzusetzen für die Bekehrung der Heiden*. Translated and edited by Klaus Fiedler and Thomas Schirrmacher. With an English list of geographical identifications (edition afem – mission classics, vol. 1). Bonn: VKW, 1993; 2nd edition 1998.

Consilia theologica Witebergensia, Das ist Wittenbergische Geistliche Rathschläge deß theuren Mannes Gottes D. Martini Lutheri, seiner Collegen and treuen Nachfolger, Frankfurt 1664.

Dann, Robert B., *Father of Faith Missions. The Life and Times of Anthony Norris Groves (1795-1853)*, Waynesboro: Authentic Media, 2004.

Dowsett, Rose, "Cooperation and the Promotion of Unity: An Evangelical Perspective" in: David A. Kerr and Kenneth R. Ross (eds), *Edinburgh 2010. Mission Then and Now*, Oxford: Regnum, 2009, pp. 250-262.

Edwards, Jonathan, *A Humble Attempt to Promote Explicit Agreement and Visible Union of God's People in Extraordinary Prayer for the Revival of Religion and the Advancement of Christ's Kingdom on Earth, Pursuant to Scripture-promises and Prophecies Concerning the Last Time*, Boston 1747.

Faix, Wilhelm, *Zinzendorf – Glaube und Identität eines Querdenkers*, Marburg: Francke, 2012.

Fiedler, Klaus, "'A Revival Disregarded and Disliked' or What do Seventh-day Adventists, Churches of Christ, Jehovah's Witnesses and the New Apostolic Church have in Common?" *Religion in Malawi* 15 (2009), pp. 10–19.

Fiedler, Klaus, "A Revival Disregarded and Disliked" in Klaus W. Müller (ed.), *Mission in fremden Kulturen*, Nürnberg: VTR, 2003.

Fiedler, Klaus, "Aspects of the Early History of the Bible School Movement", in: *Festschrift Donald Moreland. The Secret of Faith. In Your Heart - In Your Mouth*. Marthinus W. Pretorius (ed), Leuven: Evangelische Theologische Fakulteit, 1992, pp. 62-77.

Fiedler, Klaus, "Die Vielfalt der evangelischen Missionsbewegung – Der Versuch einer historischen Typologie", in: *Evangelikale Missiologie* 7 (1992), pp. 80-82.

Fiedler, Klaus, "Edinburgh 2010 and the Evangelicals", *Evangelical Theological Review*, 34/4 (Oct 2010). pp. 53-71).

Fiedler, Klaus, "It is Time to Write the History of German Speaking Evangelical Missions", in: Stephan Holthaus and Klaus W. Müller (eds.), *Die Mission der Theologie*. (Festschrift Hans Kasdorf). Bonn: VKW, 1998, pp. 136-151.

Fiedler, Klaus, "The Charismatic and Pentecostal Movements in Malawi in Cultural Perspective", *Religion in Malawi*, no. 9, 1999, pp. 28-38.

Fiedler, Klaus, *Conflicted Power in Malawian Christianity: Essays Missionary and Evangelical from Malawi*, Mzuzu: Mzuni Press 2015.

Fiedler, Klaus, *Ganz auf Vertrauen. Geschichte and Kirchenverständnis der Glaubensmissionen*, Brunnen Verlag, Giessen/Basel 1992. The book is available on the web for free download: http://tinyurl.com/fiedler.

Fiedler, Klaus, *The Making of a Maverick Missionary. Joseph Booth in Australasia*, Zomba: Kachere, 2006.

Fiedler, Klaus, *The Story of Faith Missions from Hudson Taylor to Present Day Africa"*, Oxford et al: Regnum, 1994.

Franson, Fredrik, *Profeterande Döttrar*, St Paul, 1896; Stockholm, 1897.

Franson, Fredrik, *Weissagende Töchter*, Emden 1890; also *Gemeinschaftsblatt*, Emden, no. 16 and 17, 1890.

Franz, Andreas, *Mission ohne Grenzen. Hudson Taylor und die deutschsprachigen Glaubensmissionen*, Giessen/Basel, 1993.

Frey, Reinhard, *The History of the Zambia Baptist Association*, Zomba: Kachere, 2007.

Friedrich, Bernd-Ingo, "Bruder Chingachgook. Die Herrnhuter Indianermission and Coopers Lederstrumpf-Romane," *Sächsische Heimatblätter* 4/2006, www.kulturpixel.de/artikel/3_Bruder_Chingachgook_Herrnhut_Indianermission_Cooper_Lederstrumpf.

Gensichen, Hans-Werner, "Dänisch-hallische Mission", in Gerhard Krause and Gerhard Müller (eds), *Theologische Realenzyclopädie*, vol 7, Berlin/New York 1981, pp. 319-322;

Henry, Carl F., *Basic Christian Doctrines,* Grand Rapids: Baker, 1979.

Henry, Carl F., *God, Revelation and Authority*, 6 vls, Waco: Word Books, 1983.

Hirzel, Stefan, *Der Graf und die Brüder*, Stuttgart: Quell, 1980;

Höschele, Stephan, *From the End of the World to the Ends of the Earth. The Development of Seventh-day Adventist Missiology*, Zomba: Kachere, 2004.

Isichei, Elizabeth, *A History of Christianity in Africa from Antiquity to the Present*, London: SPCK, 1995

Johnson, Todd M., Kenneth R. Ross, Sandra Lee (eds), *Atlas of Global Christianity 1910-2010*, Edinburgh University Press, 2009.

Kähler, Martin, *Schriften zu Christologie and Missiologie,* München, 1971.

Latourette, Kenneth Scott, *A History of Christianity. Beginnings to 1500*, Peabody: Prince Press, ^{7}2007 [San Francisco: Harper, 1953].

Latourette, Kenneth Scott, *A History of the Expansion of Christianity*, vol. 7, *Advance through Storm*, Grand Rapids: Zondervan, ⁵1976 (1945).

Lehmann, Arno, *Es began in Tranquebar – Die Geschichte der ersten Evangelischen Kirche in Indien*, Berlin, ²1956;

Linder, Robert D., "The Catholic Reformation" in: Tim Dowley (ed), *The History of Christianity. A Lion Handbook,* Oxford, Batavia, Sydney: Lion, 1990, pp. 410-428.

Mijoga, Hilary, *Separate but same Gospel: Preaching in African Instituted Churches in Southern Malawi*, Blantyre: CLAIM-Kachere, 2000.

Millard, J.A., "Tikhuie, Vehettge Magdalena", www.dacb.org/stories/southafrica /tikhuie_vmagdalena.html).

Miller, Basil, *Mary Slessor. Heroine of Calabar*, Minneapolis: Bethany, 1974.

Müller, Johannes, "Wie gehen Gemeinden in Europa mit kulturellen Unterschieden um?" in *Evangelikale Missiologie* 30[2014]3, pp. 135-153

Müller, Klaus, "Auf der Suche nach einem größeren Christus". Studenten-Missions-Konferenz Edinburgh/Schottland, 24.-26.6.1985. 75 Jahre nach der ersten Weltmissionskonferenz in Edinburgh 1910," *Evangelikale Missiologie*, 1986, pp. 7-13.

Ojo, Matthews, *The End-Time Army. Charismatic Movements in Modern Nigeria*, Trenton: Africa World Press, 2006.

Paas, Steven, *Johannes Rebmann. A Servant of God in Africa before the Rise of Western Colonialism*, Bonn: VKW, Nürnberg: VTR, 2011.

Palmer, Phoebe, *The Way of Holiness*, Boston, ⁵⁰1867.

Raboteau, Albert, *Slave Religion. The „Invisible Institution" in the Antebellum South*, New York: OUP, 1978.

Raupp, Werner, *Mission in Quellentexten. Von der Reformation bis zur Weltmissionskonferenz 1910*, Erlangen/Bad Liebenzell: Verlag der Evang.-Luth. Mission/Verlag der Liebenzeller Mission, 1990.

Reinke, Joost, *Deutsche Pfingstmissionen. Geschichte – Theologie – Praxis*. edition afem – mission scripts, vol. 11. Bonn: VKW, 1997.

Richter, Julius, "Die Dänisch-Hallesche Mission in ihrer Bedeutung für die evangelische Missionsgeschichte," *Allgemeine Missionszeitschrift*, 1906, pp. 301-318.

Rodney Walter, *How Europe Underdeveloped Africa*, London/Dar es Salaam 1972.

Saul, Mateyu, *An Analysis of the Rising Conflicts between Youths and Elders in Evangelical Churches: A Case of Zomba Zambezi Evangelical Church*, Zomba: Kachere, 2007.

Spener, Philip Jacob, *Pia Desideria*, trans. Theodore G. Tappert, Philadelphia: Fortress, 1964.

Strohbehn, Ulf, *Pentecostalism in Malawi: The History of the Apostolic Faith Mission*, Zomba: Kachere, 2005.

Strohbehn, Ulf, *The Zionist Churches in Malawi. History – Theology – Anthropology*, Mzuni Press, 2015.

Taylor, Howard, *By Faith. Henry W. Frost and the China Inland Mission*, Singapore, ²1988 (1938).

Wallmann, Johannes, *Philipp Jakob Spener und die Anfänge des Pietismus*, 1970.

Walls, Andrew, "Commission One and the Church's Transforming Century" in: David A. Kerr and Kenneth R. Ross (eds), *Edinburgh 2010. Mission Then and Now*, Oxford: Regnum, 2009, pp. 27-40.

Walls, Andrew, "Vom Ursprung der Missionsgesellschaften – oder: Die glückliche Subversion der Kirchen," *Evangelikale Missiologie* 1987, 35-40; 56-60, after this published in English in *Evangelical Quarterly* 88:2 (1988), pp. 141-155.

Walls, Andrew, "Three Hundred Years of Scottish Missions," in Kenneth R. Ross (ed), *Roots and Fruits. Retrieving Scotland's Missionary Story*, Oxford: Regnum, 2014.

Walls, Andrew, *The Cross-Cultural Process in Christian History*, Edinburgh: T&T Clark; New York: Orbis, 2002.

Wendland, Ernst, *Preaching that Grabs the Heart. A Rhetorical-Stylistic Study of the Chichewa Revival Sermons of Shadrack Wame*, Blantyre: CLAIM-Kachere, 2000.

Wood, A. Skevington, "Awakening" in: Tim Dowley (ed), *The History of Christianity. A Lion Handbook*, Oxford, Batavia, Sydney: Lion, 1990, pp. 436-452

Wood, A. Skevington, "The Methodists", in: Tim Dowley (ed), *The History of Christianity. A Lion Handbook*, Oxford, Batavia, Sydney: Lion, 1990, pp. 453-457.

Louise Pirouet

I dedicate this book to Louise Pirouet, who was my teacher at Makerere University (1965/66 and 1968/69), and who made me change from General Missiology to Church History, of course concentrating on Africa. When I wanted to ask her for her permission, I learnt of her death, so I think that her funeral oration is justified here. I will remember her thankfully.

Klaus Fiedler

Celebrating the Life of Louise Pirouet

Louise was a master of the short biography. She wrote 13 articles for the Oxford Dictionary of National Biography, ranging from pioneer missionaries to Idi Amin and many more in the Historical Dictionary of Uganda (a new edition incorporating much of Louise's work is in preparation). The editor of the Historical Dictionaries of Africa series described her quite simply as "one of the best authors I have worked with over these 40 years." I can hear her voice in my ear now, as I attempt to give an overview of a remarkable life, murmuring "have you cross-checked all your sources?" and "I think you need to tighten up your chronology." So hoping that she and all of you will forgive my deficiencies, I begin at the beginning:

Louise was an African by birth, as well as by love, born in Cape Town on October 4 1928 to missionary parents. The family, by this time joined by Edmund, returned to England in 1934. Louise was educated first in Aylesbury and then at the Clarendon School. She read English at Westfield College, University of London and subsequently taught at Sir William Perkin Girls School in Chertsey, before returning to the continent of her birth, with the Church Missionary Society to teach at a girls' school in Kenya. CMS did not know quite what to do with this feisty young woman and she soon found her way to the Department of Religious Studies at Makerere. Here she completed her PhD, later published as "Black Evangelists: the Spread of Christianity in Africa." This was groundbreaking research. Louise set off across Uganda in her VW beetle, interviewing the converts and catechists who planted Anglican Christianity across the country. If Louise had not carried out her research then, details of that story could well have been lost and our understanding of Ugandan Christianity impoverished. Black Evangelists remains an essential starting point for those studying the story of Christianity in Uganda and elsewhere in Africa. It is full of detail about Africans, not white missionaries, whose energy and commitment spread the faith in Uganda.

Louise was well ahead of her time—during a period when many historians were pursuing mission history in an uncritical way, she insisted that Christianity in Africa should be an African story. She was ahead of her time too in teaching, equipping and enabling her students and colleagues collecting archives, compiling a slide collection and biographical dictionary, arranging publication and organizing conferences. She was a second mother to Ugandan women students as Warden of Mary Stuart Hall and became involved in helping Sudanese refugees escaping civil war, the beginning of a life's work as passionate but eminently practical advocate for refugees. Louise returned to England in the 1970s, in time to organize relief for Ugandan Asians expelled by Idi Amin, lectured for a short time at Bishop Otter College in Chichester before a second African stint at the University of Nairobi.

Her last teaching post was at Homerton. She made a home for herself in Geldart Street and found a spiritual home here at Great St. Mary's. No. 8 was the hub and heart of Geldart Street. She had an ability to get to know anyone who moved into the street and even after she became housebound she seemed to act as a catalyst. She knew everyone in the street long before they knew each other and when there were things to be done as a street, such as getting the trees cut back, it was at her flat that they met. She was a good neighbour in all the best old fashioned senses and the whole street missed her when she left it.

Louise threw herself into the support of refugees and asylum seekers, active with organizations including Amnesty International, the Asylum Rights Campaign and Asylum Aid. She was a founder and coordinator of Charter 87. When the Home Office set up an Immigration Reception Centre in the Army Barracks at Oakington in 2000 Louise became a founder member of CamOak, a watch-dog organization to safeguard the rights of asylum seekers. She was also a key member of the Cambridge Refugee Support Group. Louise campaigned tirelessly for justice and human rights in the treatment of asylum seekers and refugees over the next ten years that the Centre was open. She spoke out fearlessly against the unfairness and inefficiency in the dealings of the Home Office and the UK Border Agency, and from a position of strength in her deep knowledge of legal matters involved with Immigration Law. She was a ceaseless and determined letter writer and had a wide network of contacts within the asylum and refugee networks and she used these to good effect when she needed to. No politician or civil servant was allowed to get away with a bland programme-forma reply or with vague promises when Louise was on the case! She also found time to write her fourth and last book, "Whatever happened to asylum in Britain."

Still there was always time for other activities and interests. Delight in her family, watching her nephews and then great nephews grow up. Support for the African Studies Centre and the Henry Martyn Centre. Students and scholars passing through Cambridge, especially those from East Africa, would find Louise always ready to share her books, her notes, her time and her hospitality. Always intellectually curious, Louise would mark up the reviews of the latest books in the Sunday supplements and TLS and was one of Heffers' best customers. She took up the history of art, following the degree course (writing the essays but not taking the exams) at Anglia Ruskin, visiting the Fitzwilliam and other galleries frequently (and when she could no longer do so, sending me to collect exhibition catalogues). She became an expert on African figures in European art and on the style of the Virgin's throne in medieval paintings.

As her illness took hold and gradually took away more and more of her physical abilities, we worried about how such an activist would cope with enforced immobility and an ever more restricted lifestyle. But Louise was in touch with her inner contemplative. Her well-stocked mind, her interest in people and events and her life of prayer sustained her to the end. She won the respect and admiration of those who cared for her so well at The Hollies. We are grateful for a gentle passing, with peace and dignity at the end. Today, we celebrate Louise a great scholar, an advocate for the vulnerable and oppressed, a wonderful sister and aunt, neighbour and friend, "a saint of the doughty variety." We celebrate her rare combination of hard head, brilliant mind, loving heart and indomitable spirit. The world is poorer for her passing but Heaven is richer.

Terry A. Barringe

Index

Africa Inland Mission 34
African Assemblies of God 40
African Independent Churches 41
AICs 41
Albigensians 17
Aldersgate 24
A-lo-pen 16
Amazon 33
America 10f, 20f, 23-27, 29, 35, 37f, 42, 50, 55
Amin, Idi 61f
Amnesty International 62
Amsterdam 38
Anabaptist 18
Anabaptist Reformation 18
Anglicans 11f, 18, 25f, 30f, 34, 39, 44, 46f, 49f, 52, 61
Angola 32
Apostles 19f, 31, 46
Apostolic Church 14f, 31, 33
Arbeitsgemeinschaft Evangelikaler Missionen 33
Arian controversies 16
Arminianism 47
Arthur`s Mission 50
Asdod 20
Asia 16-18, 42-44, 55, 62
Association of Evangelical Missions 33
Association of German Speaking Evangelical Missiologists 18, 36f
Athanasius 16
Auckland 12
Augustine 46
Australasia 12, 29
Australia 12, 20
Azores 30
Azusa Street 37
Bad Liebenzell 16, 19, 20, 22, 46
Bad Urach 16
Baghdad 30
Baptist Missionary Society 29, 34
Baptist Seminary Hamburg 7, 40, 48

Basel 14, 29f, 35, 42
Basileos 16
Baviaanskloof 21, 25
Beijing 18
Benedict of Nursia 16
Benedictines 16
Bennet, David 39
Berlin Declaration(1910) 15
Bethel 29
Beyerhaus, Professor Peter 36
Beyerhaus, Professor Peter 36
Bible Schools 34
Bible Societies 10
Biblical Theology 10
BIOLA 38
Bishops 9, 11, 16, 29, 34, 44
Black Americans 25f
Black Evangelists 61
Blantyre Revival 12
Blantyre Synod 39
Bobbio 16
Booth, Catherine 12, 50
Booth, Joseph 12, 27, 34
Booth, William 50
Brainerd, David 21
Brandl, Bernd 10
Brethren 13-15, 18, 30-35, 48, 52
Brierley, Leslie 51
British Library 28
Brussels 42
Bulstrode (UK) 13
Bultmann, Rudolf 40
Caldwell, Rev Robert 29
California 19, 38f
Californian Indians 39
Calvin, John 19, 46
Canon Law 25
Cape Town 14, 61
Capitalism 38
Carey, William 9, 12, 27-29, 34, 46, 51f
Carmelite 19
Catholic Reformation 19
Central Asia 44
Centre of all Theology 7
Centre of the Bible 8

Chad 30
Change of Denomination 30
Chicago 49
Chicago Avenue Church 49
Children of Revivals 9f, 16, 44
China 7, 16, 18, 32-36, 42, 44, 49
China Inland Mission 32, 34-36, 44
Chinese 7, 16, 34, 55
Chirwa, Frank 17
Christendom 11, 52
Christian and Missionary Alliance 15
Christian Brethren 14, 30f, 35
Christian Churches 14, 43
Christian Diversity 10, 14, 32
Christian Mission in Many Lands (CMML) 33
Christian Pluralism 10, 53
Christian Unity 14, 25, 32, 42, 45, 51, 53
Church Missionary Society 11, 33, 43, 61
Church of England 11, 26
Church of Jesus Christ of the Latter Day Saints 15
Church of South India 13
Church of the East 16
Church Union 13, 45, 52
Church Unity 9, 52
Churches of Christ 14-16, 31f
Cistercians 16
Citeaux 16
Class 13, 39
Clergy 12
Cluny 16
Columbus 18
Communism 38
Concept of the Church 9, 43-45
Congo 32, 42
Congo Basin 33
Congo Inland Mission 34
Congregationalist 7, 27
Contarini 19
Conversion 7-10, 14, 18f, 22-24, 27, 31, 34, 36, 47, 49, 52, 54, 55
Copperbelt 32
Council of Churches 14, 38, 43f

Countess of Huntingdon 25
Cross Life 40
Crusade 17
Cultural Revolution 7, 42
Danish-Halle Mission 21, 23
Darby, John Nelson 31f
Decline 15f, 22, 26, 32, 38, 40, 45f
Denmark 22, 53
Deutsche Ostasienmission 23
Deutscher Frauenmissionsgebetsbund 35
Disciples 8, 12, 14, 20, 32, 40
Doll, Ludwig 10, 27
Dominic 17f
Dominicans 16-18
Dong, Mao Dse 7
Double Predestination 46
Dowie, Alexander 15
Dr McIntire 36
Dr Palmer, Walter 50
Durham University 30
Dutch Reformed Church in the Cape 21f
East London Training Institute for Evangelists at Home and Abroad 34
Ecclesiastical Office 9, 25
Ecclesiastical Tradition 13
Ecclesiola in Ecclesia 24
Ecumenical 9, 14, 33, 35-37, 44, 53
Edinburgh 1910 14, 33, 37, 42-45, 51f
Edwards, Jonathan 9, 23, 26, 47
Eigenständigkeit 36
Ekwendeni Mission 54
Elder Amaro 51
Elliot, John 21
England 11, 18, 22f, 25f, 29, 61f
Enlightenment 21-23, 38
Essenius 22
Evangelical Alliance 13, 35
Evangelical Church in Malawi 39
Evangelical Church of Guinea-Bissau 50
Evangelical Graduate School of Missions 36
Evangelical Revival 12, 14, 30
Evangelical Theological Faculty in Leuven 13, 22, 35, 42, 47

Evangeline Booth 50
Evangelism 8, 32, 34
Evangelists 12f, 24f, 34, 61
Evangelization 11, 19, 25, 27, 30, 42, 44, 49
Exclusive Brethren 32
Extraordinary Officers of the Church 20
Extremes 7, 9, 13, 15, 17, 28, 31, 36, 41, 53
Faith Missions 9, 12-14, 27, 29-36, 43
Fellowship Movements 15, 36
Fellowship of Youth 39
Folk Church 14, 16, 54
Forum Wiedenest 33
Fourah Bay College 30
France 30
Franciscans 16f
Frankfurt 20, 24, 46
Franson, Frederick 49
Franz, Andreas 35, 42
Frederic the Great 23
Free Churches 36
Free Evangelical 53
Free Methodists 13, 34
Free Will 45f
Freetown 27
Fricker, Bessie 13, 50
Friedenshort Mission 35
Fuller 38
Fuller, Elder 27, 46
Fundamentalists 38
Gabriel, Andrew 12
Genadendal 21, 25
General Baptists 26
George Whitefield 24, 47
German Liberal Theology 32
Germany 13f, 18, 21f, 24, 29, 32f, 37, 42, 46, 48f, 54f
Glaubensmissionen 10, 14, 35, 42
Gospels 7f, 11, 17, 19, 30, 34, 41, 50, 51, 53f
Great Awakening 5, 9, 11, 15, 22-26, 28-30, 33, 38-40, 42f, 53
Great Century 27
Great Commission 20

Groves, Anthony Norris 31f
Grubb, Norman 50f
Guinea Bissau 13, 50
Guinness, Fanny 34
Guinness, Grattan 12, 34
Hall, Nellie 13, 49
Halle University 8
Hamburg Brethren Assembly 48
Healing 13, 15, 41f
Health, Power and Wealth 41
Heretics 17f
Hermannsburg 29
Hermits 16
Holiness 12-14, 24, 33f, 39, 50
Holiness Revival 12, 30, 33f, 36f
Holy Land 17
Holy Spirit 9, 12, 16, 23, 28, 39, 48f, 55
Home Cell 24
Hoornbeek, Johannes 22
House Church Movement 48
Huntingdon Connexion 25
Hyper-Calvinists 40
ICCC 36
Ignatius of Loyola 19
Imminent Return of Christ 14
India 13, 18, 31
Indians 19, 21
Inner Asia 17
Innovative 19, 24f, 28, 32, 34, 40, 42, 51
Inquisition 18
Integration of the Missions into the Church 11
Interchurch Aid 12
International Missionary Council 43f
Irish Monasticism 16
Irish Monks 16
Irving, Edward 31
Japan 16
Jehovah`s Witnesses 15, 31
Jerusalem 44
Jesuits 19
Jesus 8f, 11-13, 15, 19, 22f, 52f
Jews 19, 51
John of Montecorvino 18
Kähler, Martin 8

Kampala 7
Katharoi 18
Kawamba, Bright 12
Kenya 13, 61
Keswick 14
Kinshasa 42
Korntal 36
Krapf 11
Kuruman 7, 29, 47
Kwang Sin Basin 35
Kweichow Province 35
Ladies of Wisdom 11
Laity 12, 24, 40
Latin America 37, 43, 55
Latourette, Kenneth Scott 9-11, 15, 18, 22, 27, 37f, 46
Lausanne Movement 14
Liberal Theology 23, 32
Liberation 7, 19, 23
Lima Document 9
Lima Process 13, 52
Living Waters 41
Livingstone Inland Mission 34
London Missionary Society 29
London Zoo 30
Los Angeles 37
Lusaka Baptist Church 48
Luther, Martin 19f, 24, 39, 46
Lutheran 7, 18, 21, 39, 46, 53
Magangani, Fanuel 12
Makerere University 7, 46, 61
Malawi 10-12, 27, 29f, 32, 34, 37, 39-41, 46, 54
Man as a Rational Being 22
Mao Tse Tung 7
Mary of Egypt 16
Mary Stuart Hall 62
Matrilineal 7
Mau Mau 13
Mendicant Orders 16
Mennonite Brethren 18
Mercator Projection 47f
Methodist Societies 24f, 49
Methodists 25f, 35, 40, 49
Mexican 19

Migration 45, 54f, 62
Miller, William (1782-1849) 31
Mission Halls 34
Mission Societies 11, 15, 53
Missional Church 9
Missionary Society 11, 28f, 33f, 43, 61
Missions at Home 10
Missionshaus Bibelschule Wiedenest 33
Modalities 11
Moe, Malla 13
Moffat, Mary 7, 29
Moffat, Robert 7, 47, 29
Monasticism 16
Monte Cassino 16
Montfort Fathers 11
Moody, Dwight Lyman 12, 48f
Moravian 21f, 24, 30
Mormons 15
Mott, John 44, 51
Mozambique 12
Mrs Baxter 13
Müller, George 31f
Muslims 17, 43
Nadere Reformatie 22
National Socialism 38
Native Americans 21
Near East 16
Nestorians 16
Netherlands 18, 22, 30, 55
Neuendettelsau 29
Neukirchen Mission 10, 27
New Apostolic Church 15, 31, 33
New Delhi 1961 11, 44
New Organizations 9f
New Testament 8, 13-15, 31
Ngoni 41
Nightingale, Florence 26
Northern Africa 33
Nuns 16
Open Brethren 32
Oratory of Divine Love 19
Ordained 12, 14, 25, 29, 35
Ordination 12, 16, 21, 25, 29, 31f, 35
Ordination of the Pierced Hands 12
Örebro Mission 40

Organic Unity 13
Orthodox 39
Orthodox Churches 16
Orthodox Theologians 7, 19-22, 46
Our Lady of Africa Prayer Group 40
Paas, Steven 11
Pachom 16
Painting of the First Fruits 2
Palestrina 19
Palmer, Phoebe 13, 50
Parochial Principle 47, 54
Particular Baptists 26, 52
Pastora 51
Pastors 13, 21f, 25, 27, 46, 51
Paul 15, 20
Paul III 19
Pentecostals 14f, 37, 39, 52
Personal Faith 8, 10, 13f
Peters Projection 47
Peters, George W. 18
Phillip 20
Pia Desideria 24
Pietism 22f
Pietists 24
Pilkington, George 29
Pirouet, Louise 7, 29, 61
Plymouth Brethren 15
Pommerania 13
Pope Innocent III 17
Popes 18, 20, 46
Portuguese 19, 50
Poverty 16f, 26
Power for Service 14
Praise Team 40
Prämillennial 14
Predestination 45-47
Presbyterian 7, 18, 20, 54
Presuppositions 30
Princeton University 28
Prison Reform 10, 26
Professor Peter Beyerhaus 36
Professor Walls 11, 28f, 45
Prophetic Movement 14, 31
Protestant 9, 18f, 22, 29, 35, 37, 39, 53, 55

Punch 30
Puritan Revival 19, 22, 40
Puritanism 22
Puritans 19
Race 13, 23, 29, 46, 49
Rationalism 22
Rebmann 11
Reformations 18-20, 22, 39, 46
Reformed 18, 21f, 53
Reformed Baptists 39, 46, 48
Religious Geography 23
Religious Orders 11, 16, 18f
Renaissance 18
Renewal 16, 39f
Restorationist Revival 13-15, 31f, 34, 36
Returnees 27
Revelation 8, 38
Revival Characteristics 12
Ritchie, Bruce 7, 29, 47
Rivers of Life Evangelical Church 39
Rodney, Walter 27
Role of Women 17, 32, 45
Roman Catholic 11, 17, 30, 37, 39f, 55
Rostock 21
Rwanda 30
Sacraments 10, 14, 24f, 44, 52
Salvation 8, 13f, 24, 46-48, 53
Salvation Army 50
Sanctification experience 14, 23
Scotland 18, 26
Scottish Common Sense Philosophy 32
Second Recession 18
Senegal 51
Seventh-day Adventist Church 15, 17, 28, 31-33
Shungking in Szechwan Province 35
Sierra Leone 27, 30
Silk Road 18
Simeon, Charles 26
Singapore 13, 35
Slave Religion 25
Slave Trade 10, 13, 27
Slavery 13, 27
Slessor, Mary 29
Social Differences 13

Socialism 38, 53
Society for the Propagation of the Gospel 11
Sodalities 11, 16f, 22
South Africa 7, 29
South Africa General Mission 47
South Tyrol 16
Spanish 19
Spener, Philipp Jakob 24
Spurgeon, Charles Haddon 12, 47
Spurgeon, Thomas 12, 47
Sri Lanka 45
St. Anthony's 16
St. Clara 16
St. Francis 16, 17
St. Gallen 16
St. Thomas 13, 25
Stone/Campbell Revival 31
Student Christian Movement 44
Student Volunteer Movement 15, 44
Successor of the Apostles 20, 46
Sudan Belt 33, 43
Sudan Interior Mission 34
Sudan Pionier Mission 34
Sultan in Egypt 17
Surinam 30, 35
Swaziland 13
Sweden 40, 49
Switzerland 16, 18, 55
Tabernacle 12
Tambaram (1938) 44
Tasmania 12
Taylor, Hudson 12f, 34f, 42
Taylor, Maria 34
Tellinck, J. 22
Teresa of Avila 19
Theocratic Organization 15
Threefold Office 9, 52
Timbuktu 30
Tranquebar 21, 23
Trinity 38
Tswana 7, 29, 47
Tübingen 20
Typology 9
Uganda 29f, 61f

Undelimited Identity 36, 45
Unevangelized Territories 19
Unevangelized Tribes Mission 34
Unitarians 26, 40
Unity 13f, 16, 25, 31f, 35, 42-45, 51-55
University of Nairobi 62
Unreached 19, 33f, 43
Valdensians 18
Valdes, Peter 17
van Koevering, Mark 12
Van Lodenstein 22
Van Nuys (California) 39
Vanguards of African Culture 41
Virtuosity Digest 30
Voetius, Gisbertus 22
Voltaire 23
Von Bülow 13
Von Schurman, Anna Maria 22
Von Thiele-Winkler, Eva 35
Vow of poverty 16, 17
Walls, Andrew F. 11, 28f, 45
Walton, Spencer 47
Warneck, Gustav 11, 36
WEC 13, 51
Wesley, John 23-26, 46f, 49
Wheaton 38
White Fathers 11
White Sisters 11
Wholistic Mission 45, 54
Wilberforce, William 13, 27
Wittenberg 20, 39, 46
Women 12, 16f, 22, 25, 29, 31, 35, 45, 48-51, 61
Women and Men 12, 24, 50
Women Preachers 26, 49f
World Council of Churches 14, 38, 43f
World Students Christian Federation 15
Wuppertal 53
Xavier, Francis 19
Zambezi Evangelical Church 36, 39f
Zambia 32, 46, 48
Zeist 30
Zinzendorf 13, 21
Zinzendorf, Nikolaus Count of 13
Zomba Baptist Church 41

www.ingramcontent.com/pod-product-compliance
Lightning Source LLC
Chambersburg PA
CBHW071415300426
44114CB00016B/2305